Black Pawl

Ben Ames Williams

Nabu Public Domain Reprints:

You are holding a reproduction of an original work published before 1923 that is in the public domain in the United States of America, and possibly other countries. You may freely copy and distribute this work as no entity (individual or corporate) has a copyright on the body of the work. This book may contain prior copyright references, and library stamps (as most of these works were scanned from library copies). These have been scanned and retained as part of the historical artifact.

This book may have occasional imperfections such as missing or blurred pages, poor pictures, errant marks, etc. that were either part of the original artifact, or were introduced by the scanning process. We believe this work is culturally important, and despite the imperfections, have elected to bring it back into print as part of our continuing commitment to the preservation of printed works worldwide. We appreciate your understanding of the imperfections in the preservation process, and hope you enjoy this valuable book.

BLACK PAWL

BY THE SAME AUTHOR

EVERED

*The Story of the
Famous Red Bull*

"I have read all of the novels of Ben Ames Williams, and I like them all. But surely 'Evered' is his best thus far. I read this through from first page to last without leaving my chair. It's a powerful story."—WILLIAM LYON PHELPS.

E. P. DUTTON & COMPANY

BY
BEN AMES WILLIAMS
AUTHOR OF "EVERED"

NEW YORK
E. P. DUTTON & COMPANY
681 FIFTH AVENUE

Copyright, 1922,
By E. P. Dutton & Company

All Rights Reserved

PRINTED IN THE UNITED
STATES OF AMERICA

BLACK PAWL

CHAPTER I

SPIESS, a born lubber who would never learn the way of the sea, bungled his simple share of the task of getting the mate's boat away. Black Pawl, master of the schooner, was near by; and he cuffed the man. The buffet was good-natured enough, and Black Pawl laughed as he administered it. Nevertheless it knocked Spiess end over end. The man got up, grumbling; and Red Pawl, the captain's son and mate, said sharply to his father:

"I'll handle my boat and my men, sir. Let them be."

Black Pawl laughed again. "Fiddle, boy," he retorted. "If you knew your job, you'd have Spiess trained before this. He's been thirty months on your hands."

"Keep your fists off my men," Red Pawl repeated sullenly; and Black Pawl frowned.

"Get your boat away," he ordered. "And stop your mouth."

They had worked into the bay that morning, threading the intricate passages between the islands and the reefs with a familiarity that showed Black Pawl knew his way about. Not that the passage was difficult. There was always room, and to spare; but an ignorant man might well have taken a short way through blue water and piled up on a slumbering reef. Black Pawl was not ignorant, not ignorant where these waters were concerned. He had made this anchorage a full score of times, in his years upon the sea.

Where the schooner now lay, there was a beauty all about them, the unmeasured and profligate beauty of the tropics that appealed to every sense a man possessed. The eye was drunk with it; the air was richly heavy with a fragrance that caressed the nostrils; the stirring currents of this air brought faint, far bird-songs, and the musical tones of the natives, and blended them in a symphony to which the murmuring sea lent undertone. The touch of the sun and of the sun-warmed wind was as caressing as the touch of a woman's hand. And to the fifth sense of men hardened to salt-horse and the rough fare of the sea, the fruit the natives brought was delight unutterable. Beauty made for the eye, the ear, the nose, the hand, the tongue—this lay all about them.

The islands were picturesque, densely wooded, and pleasantly broken by steep cliffs and reaches of bare rock. They had an appearance of permanence and strength that was welcome to eyes which had looked too long on coral atolls that barely topped the sea. The bay where the schooner lay was perfectly sheltered. A mile away, the beach lay white as silver snow. To right and left, protecting horns of land came down steeply to the water, and were wooded to the rippling edge. Along the beach were ranged a few native houses, all but hidden among the orange trees and the palms. Those who had seen it will know the spot—the Vau Vau group, ten miles or so from what passed for the "town."

The native canoes were swarming out toward the schooner, the islanders laughing and calling like children—like amiable children, anxious to make friends. Their narrow dugouts with the balancing outrigger were deeply loaded with enough fruit and provender for a fleet. There was no need to barter for food. Once the islanders saw that the schooner was friendly, the stuff was heaped aboard. Huge oranges, great bunches of gold and green bananas, cocoanuts by the cluster, a fowl or two. One man laughingly slung aboard a pig, its feet trigged fast with strands of fiber; and it lay in the waist and squealed and squealed, kicking helplessly where it lay.

These were unspoiled folk; they lived in a land of plenty, flowing with what passed for milk and honey. But there were no pearls, no treasures to bring the traders flocking here—nothing but the abundant food. They told Black Pawl, in their broken tongue, that no vessel had anchored in this bay for three years past. They were unqualifiedly delighted to make the schooner welcome and help her take aboard the wood and water which she needed for the homeward voyage, just beginning. They wore loose folds of a cloth made of bark, this scant garb supplemented here and there by shirts or trousers of obviously Occidental origin. The women and the children stayed in the canoes; and no man came aboard the schooner without first donning some such garment of civilization. Many of the men knew Black Pawl; and they stood before him—he had taken his post at the break of the quarterdeck, and looked kindly down upon them—and told him many things, many bits of news of themselves and of the islands. Red Pawl and the second mate, each with his boat, had gone ashore for water and for wood.

One thing they told Black Pawl which led him to question them at length; and when he knew all they could tell him, he took his glass and watched the beach, a mile away, where his son had landed. A tall islander pointed out to him a flutter of white, a woman's skirt. He nodded, and watched, and saw the woman, and a black-garbed man, approach Red Pawl and talk with him. He lowered his glass and continued to question the natives, with an occasional glance toward the beach.

Some of the younger men from the island were investigating the schooner, clustering here and there at the sharp cries of wonder and surprise which were uttered when some adventurer made a new and more marvelous discovery. Yet the *Deborah Hoar* was not remarkable. A two-masted whaler with full casks after close on three years in the South Pacific, she was dingy with the smoke and soot that marred her canvas, and her hull bore the hard marks of wear. Now all the canvas was down and furled, except the mainsail. They would be working out again this afternoon—no need of lowering that. The decks were scrubbed white, and reasonably clear of the litter of gear which, seemingly disorderly, yet is the height of order.

The blacks studied the big windlass and bitts, forward; they climbed over and around the cold try-works; they peered down the main hatch and adventured into the fo'c'stle, and admired from a respectful distance the three long whaleboats on the bearers along either rail, and on skids at the stern. These boats, tools of the *Deborah's* epic trade, were almost half as long as the schooner herself. They were, moreover, as seaworthy as many a larger craft; and save only perhaps the dory of the fishing-fleet, they would outride any other type of small-boat that white men know. The two at the rails were just abeam the break in the deck; the stern boat lay crosswise, lashed in place upon the skids. A larger craft of the *Deborah's* sort would have had one or two spare boats stowed on the boathouse just forward of the mizzenmast; but the *Deborah's* spares, if she had had any, would have been athwartship, on the skids, aft. As it was, she had none. The third mate and his boat had been lost in the killing of the last whales; and the schooner was going home with only two officers besides Black Pawl. The third mate's widow in Nantucket would get his lay, along with his seachest and the sparse belongings in his cabin.

Black Pawl saw his son's boat put off at last from the beach and start for the schooner. He roared good-humoredly at the blacks and drove them overside. They went, giggling and laughing. Black Pawl was a tall, lean man, with a big framework of bones insufficiently covered with flesh. Nevertheless there was strength in his stringy arms and his lank legs and his gaunt torso. He had got his name of *Black* instead of *Dan* Pawl in the days when his head was crowned with a shock of ebony; now that shock of hair was iron gray, almost white. Beneath it, the bold, black eyes of the man gazed mockingly at the world. He was known for a bold man, and a cold one; he laughed much, but when he laughed, it was as though he mocked himself and all the world. He had suffered; his face told that. He still suffered; the mark of it was alive in his eyes. There were whispers about him—at which he laughed.

His son, Red Pawl—they had been christened so by the men of the sea, for it was necessary to have a mark that would distinguish one from the other—his son was his opposite. Three inches shorter than his father, and reputed to be thrice as strong, he was red of hair, red of countenance, morose and sullen in speech— an unsmiling man. Whereas Black Pawl had friends everywhere, and enemies everywhere, Red Pawl had no friends and no enemies; but men disliked and avoided him, and wondered why Black Pawl had him about. "I'd break his neck—even if he were my son," they said. Black Pawl told some one, once, in a jocular mood, that Red was a penance. "I bear him like the load of my sins about my neck," he said, and laughed his mirthless laugh.

There had always been enmity between father and son. Red was in his twenties now; Black Pawl was close to fifty. And for three months past, Red had been taking occasion to balk his father, to come between Black Pawl and the men, to seek strife. At such times, Black Pawl laughed at him; but when he was alone, and thought upon the matter, he frowned with a weary anxiety. If it had been another man, Black Pawl would have destroyed him and had done with it. Yet it was not because Red was his son that he held his hand; it was some stronger feeling. He disliked Red, son or no son, as much as the others did. There may have been some truth in the reason for his forbearance which he had given, when he spoke—laughingly —of his own sins. It is a hard and ugly thing for a father to recognize his own evil self in his son.

Red Pawl's boat was nearing the schooner. It drove in a hair line, deviating no whit; and the natives in the canoes scattered before it with shrieks of laughing consternation. One was slow. The whaleboat sheared away the outrigger, and the canoe spun around and filled. Red called over his shoulder:

"Keep clear, there, you swine!"

But it was hardly worth while to swear at these islanders. They shouted with mirth at the misadventure; a trio of paddlers hauled the occupants of the wrecked canoe into their own craft; and Red Pawl's boat slid alongside the *Deborah*.

Black Pawl, on the quarter, saw that the man and the woman were in Red's boat. The man was elderly, clothed in black. The Captain knew the breed of the church. The woman, he saw, was young.

Red and his boat-steerer steadied the boat while the missionary climbed to the deck. He reached down and took the girl by both hands, and she stepped lightly up to a place by his side. Red said morosely:

"Ask Cap'n Pawl."

The missionary looked aft and saw Black Pawl on his quarterdeck. He turned to the girl, and smiled, and said: "Come!"

They walked side by side toward the starboard deck-steps. Black Pawl studied them as they approached, but made no move to meet them. The missionary stood aside to let the girl climb to the quarter, then followed her and approached Black Pawl. He was an old man, with white hair and kindly eyes and lips; a man mellowed by right living and right thinking; a broad man, without cant and without guile. This was written plain in his face; but that spirit of mockery which lived in Black Pawl moved him to say in greeting:

"Good morning, Father!"

He knew quite well that this missionary was not of that church which is father and mother to her people; he also knew that clergy of another cloth, if they are meanly made, resent the appellation he had given this man. But the missionary only smiled and said in his gentle, firm tones without a note of pique:

"Good morning, Cap'n Pawl."

And by this Black Pawl knew him for a man, and thrust out his big hand. They gripped.

"My name is Samuel Poor," the missionary said; "and this is Ruth Lytton."

He gestured toward the girl; and Black Pawl,

turning, saw her at close range, and his heart for an instant stood still.

She was tall and strongly made, and sweetly. Further, she was beautiful. But there was something else in her face, and in her eyes, which pierced the Captain's consciousness. For an instant his face was a mask of tragedy. The missionary was looking at the girl, and did not see; but the girl saw and was troubled.

Then Black Pawl smiled. There was beauty in the man when he smiled—beauty, and the radiance of strength, and the glory of audacity. He took her hand.

"Ruth—Lytton?" he repeated.

"Yes," said the missionary. The girl studied this tall man who held her hand; and because she was brave, she asked him:

"Why were you—unhappy when you saw me?"

"Unhappy?" Black Pawl flung back his head and laughed. "I am never unhappy. There is nothing worth unhappiness."

"Why?" she repeated.

His eyes met hers evenly; and a spark flashed

between them. He touched her hand, which he still held, with his left, then dropped it.

"You are like some one I have known," he said almost as if to himself, "—a little. That was my first thought. It is gone now. I was wrong. A fancy that comes to me often! The notion that the women I meet are—like some one I have known."

He turned to the missionary, and the girl stepped back a little—but still watching him, as though she could not take her eyes away from him. Yet this was not strange, for Black Pawl was a man whom men and women anywhere would stop to look at twice. He asked the missionary now:

"What can I do for you?"

"Miss Lytton and I want passage home with you."

Black Pawl chuckled. "There are passenger ships touching at the Islands. Why choose the *Deborah?*"

"It should be cheaper," said the missionary. "We have not the money for the more expensive way."

"How do you know it will be cheaper?"

"We count on your good nature, Cap'n Pawl."

Himself an audacious man, the Captain admired audacity in others.

"You have courage, sir," he said.

"I know men," was the missionary's quiet reply.

"Where are your belongings?"

"On the beach."

"I'll send for them."

The missionary smiled. "No need for you to send," he said. "I will—"

He stepped to the rail and called to the nearest canoe. Half a dozen thrust toward the schooner, and the missionary spoke to the men in them. They darted shoreward, racing. The missionary looked after them, his eyes shaded beneath the wide brim of his hat. Other canoes pressed together below him, and he talked cheerily to their occupants. A woman began to wail, and the missionary called down reassurance to her.

The girl turned to the Captain, who had watched the little scene with her.

"They love him," she commented. "They are sorry he is going away."

A man saw her, and grinning, shouted something; she smiled and lifted her hand.

"They love you, too," Black Pawl said. "That is easy seen."

She nodded. "Yes," she replied. "And I them."

The Captain studied her with a sidelong glance, measuring her profile, and marking the shape of forehead and of eye; and upon his face that tragic mask again descended. But when she turned toward him, he flung it off with a laugh. They leaned against the rail side by side, talking idly.

About the schooner the canoes threaded their expert way. Amidships, stores of wood were coming aboard. The second mate's boat approached the *Deborah,* towing casks of water. Red Pawl set men to rig tackle to swing the casks aboard. The gear creaked as the booms swung back and forth with each lift and fall of the schooner beneath them. Above their heads the mainsail flapped. The cries of the islanders rose softly, their musical tones smothering the harsh commands of the mate.

The second mate's boat was nearing. With her eyes upon it, the girl asked:

"Who is the officer in that boat?"

"Dan Darrin," Black Pawl told her, "my second mate. A fine boy." He chuckled teasingly. "And you're rosy already, at the sight of him."

"I'm not," she denied, her cheeks refuting her denial.

"A fine boy," declared Black Pawl again.

CHAPTER II

THEY did not get away as soon as the Captain had expected. Before coming to this anchorage, the oil-casks had been securely stowed against the homeward voyage; the whaling gear had been taken out of the boats and cleaned and oiled and sent below. The rigging was set up and tarred down, and the hull and spars were scraped and painted to suit even Black Pawl's exacting eye. With the last stores aboard, the schooner was ready for sea; but toward midafternoon the weather-signs became unfavorable, and it was decided to lie where they were until whatever weather was brewing should have blown itself out. The narrow outlet from the bay was no place in which to be caught by a squall.

When this word of the Captain's went forward, the men gathered in knots upon the deck, talking together; and Black Pawl saw his son and mate speak to one or two. He was not surprised, therefore, when a group of the men presently came aft and stopped at the break of the deck to speak to him. With Red Pawl behind him and Dan Darrin at one side, he looked down on them. The missionary and the girl were aft by the wheel.

"Well, what now?" Black Pawl asked good-humoredly.

"We'm heard you'll lay here till the wind's fit, sir," declared the spokesman.

"Yes. Object?"

The man grinned. "Not us, sir. But—what about a break ashore? Get the kinks out of our legs."

"And get the kinks into your head, eh?" Black Pawl chuckled. "Drown yourselves in some native rot-gut?"

The man looked sheepish. "The mate were thinking you'd leave us go."

"The mate were thinking, were he?" Black Pawl mimicked. "Then why come to me?"

The man shifted uneasily from one foot to the other. Black Pawl looked toward his son. "What's the matter, Red?" he asked.

"I told them it was fair they should go," Red

Pawl answered, dourly, "that there was no reason you should object."

"What if I object without reason?"

"That's despotism!"

Black Pawl laughed aloud. "Where did you learn that word?"

"You've taught it to me."

The Captain's smile upon his son became terrible; but when he turned to the men, his voice was level and without emotion. "There's no reason you should not go," he said, and they cheered. "Except that I'll not let you!" he added grimly. "Get forward, you swipes. And look sharp."

They hesitated an instant, even then, in stupefaction at the overthrow of their sudden hopes; then they fell to mumbling among themselves. Dan Darrin took a step forward to his Captain's side, as though to support him; but Black Pawl needed no help to enforce his orders.

"Sharp, I say!" he cried cheerfully, and he leaped among them, his long arms flailing. He struck with the open hand, but those whom he struck fell; and others fell in their flurry to escape him. In a matter of seconds the deck was clear to the try-works, save for the harpooners by the starboard rail, who laughed at the crew's discomfiture. Once safely forward, the men grinned too. Black Pawl had the strange faculty of commanding a liking even from those over whom he tyrannized. When he came aft, his eye lighted on his son, and he asked gently:

"Now, was that not unreasonable despotism?"

Red Pawl replied sullenly: "Yes."

His father's eyes twinkled. "Louder," he enjoined, "—so that your audience, yonder, may hear." And he asked again: "Was not that brutal tyranny?"

His son's eyes blazed morosely now. "Yes, brutal, and be damned to you!" he bellowed; and his voice carried the length of the schooner.

"So!" said Black Pawl. "You've got the effect you were after—my son. You're the hero, defending them against my unjust fists. Be satisfied!"

The son gave the father eye for eye. "You're a brave man—and a damned rash man," he said.

"Fiddle!" Black Pawl replied. "If you mean what you seem to mean, and if you had the sap of a man, you'd strike now. You'll never make an omelet, Red, my boy. You're too squeamish about breaking eggs."

He turned, with that, and strode toward the missionary and the girl; and at the same instant Dan Darrin caught Red's eye, and the two stood for a moment in a wordless and motionless conflict. In that clash of eyes, Dan Darrin told the mate that he was the Captain's man; and Red Pawl understood, and made no sign, but turned away.

They made out of the bay the third day after, the homeward-bound pennant flying. The wooded shores slid past them, lush green beneath the sun; and as dusk came on, they dropped the islands behind them, and the sudden night of the tropics came down. Overhead, the stars. Darrin and the girl were on the quarter-deck together. Once in the open sea, Black Pawl and his son had gone below. Ruth liked Dan Darrin. She liked Black Pawl. She liked the harpooners —liked every man aft, save perhaps the Captain's son. Red Pawl was a hard man to like, on any count. But the others were her friends.

Darrin, however, already held a place apart. They were within a few years of the same age;

he was an honest, four-square man with a clear eye, and she was a girl, and beautiful. Perhaps it lay in that. They looked out across the sea, this night, and up at the stars. The stars in southern seas are nearer and more intimate than in our northern latitude. It is as if the veil of our smoky atmosphere were drawn aside; and they ride the heavens for us clear and unobscured. The eye more easily penetrates the vast reaches of infinity; and the stars appear in orderly perspective, less like luminous pin-holes in a deep, blue board. Dan Darrin spoke of this to the girl; and she replied that she had never seen them otherwise.

"You mean you were born out here? Never been back home?"

"I was born back home," she told him. "But I was only a baby when we came out here,—my mother and I,—you see. So I don't remember."

He wanted to ask her more. Where was "back home"? He knew her name; but what lay behind her name? He was eager to read each chapter and each page of her Book of Life. But something—perhaps it was her own reticence— held his tongue.

Another had wondered with him—Red Pawl. The first mate had a hot eye for a woman, beautiful or not. And this woman was beautiful. He had watched her sidewise, from the beginning; he had asked herself about herself. She told him nothing; and he went to the old missionary, who told him no more than nothing. "She and her mother lived on the island, near me," he said. "When her mother died, last spring, she came to me. I saw she must go back to her kind. So—we are going. That is all."

"Running away?" Red Pawl suggested maliciously. "Why? What from?"

The missionary looked at him steadily. "From men unfit to look upon her," he said; and Red Pawl, in spite of himself, was abashed, and let the matter lie.

When, on this night, he missed Darrin and the girl, he went on deck and found them, and the stars. So he gave Darrin a task to do, thinking to have the girl to himself. But she went below as soon as Darrin left her, in spite of Red Pawl's suggestion that she keep the deck with him.

When she was gone, the first mate paced back and forth for a space, then fell to talking with the man at the wheel. They talked in undertones, as though afraid of being heard.

Next day they threw the try-works overside, brick by brick. The crew made it an occasion of rejoicing. It meant the hard and dangerous toil of the whale-fisheries was over and done with; it meant home, and money to spend, and a few weeks ashore. They shouted and sang at the business of dismantling the ovenlike structure where so many flenches of blubber had been boiled to scrapple for the oil they yielded. The men vied in hurling the bricks, to see which might throw one farthest out across the water. They shied half-bricks at the birds that still followed them from the islands they had left.

When the last brick was gone, the big pots were lowered into the holds and made secure; the chimney and the firebox were stowed away; and the broad pan which is always full of water when the pots are going, so that the deck may not be charred, was scoured and put in its place. Remained only the littered deck where the try-works had been. This they scrubbed till the deck-planking was white as a bleached bone. And they sang at the work, for the day was fine, and the wind was fair, and they were putting behind them the seas where they had toiled.

Black Pawl shouted at them, jovially abusive; and Dan Darrin lent a hand when another strong hand was needed now and then; Red Pawl scowled from the rail, and cursed them when they lagged. The old missionary and the girl watched all this, as they followed all the life of the schooner, from the quarter. To be at sea on such days was to the girl bliss and poetry and joy unspeakable. She told Dan Darrin so when he came aft. "It's beautiful," she cried. "So fine, and big! I don't think I should ever tire of the sea."

Black Pawl heard, and laughed, and called to her: "You'll have chance enough to learn. You'll get your fill of it before the end. We'll not touch land from now till we make home harbor, child."

She nodded, accepting what he said as true. And he meant it so; but as matters turned out, when Black Pawl said they would not touch land again, he was wrong.

CHAPTER III

THUS far fair weather had followed them from the island; the schooner laid the leagues of ocean behind her and plunged steadfastly along the homeward course. There was peace aboard her; the men were cheerful, and the cabin was quiet. Red Pawl said little, and what speech he held was generally with the men at the wheel, with whom he talked at times in furtive undertones; but if Black Pawl remarked this,—and the Captain's eyes did not miss much that passed aboard his craft,—he made no sign.

The missionary was interested in Black Pawl. He had heard, on the island, certain dark stories of the man; yet he found the captain of the *Deborah* a good companion, intelligent, reasonably jovial, and courteous enough. He sought on two or three occasions to talk with him, but in the beginning Black Pawl had put him off, half avoiding him, it seemed, as if he were unwilling to be alone with a man of the church. The missionary was used to reading men; he said in his thoughts: "There is a trouble upon Black Pawl's soul." He wondered whether he might help the man, and so sought his friendship and his confidence.

He saw, after a time, that Black Pawl constantly watched Ruth Lytton without seeming to do so; it was obvious that he liked to talk to her. He saw, also, that after such talks with the girl the Captain was more often than not restless and at greater outs with the world.

It was on the quarter-deck, one night when the moon was full and high, that the missionary found Black Pawl alone. He did not thrust himself upon the other, but took the rail across the deck and ignored the man. Joining him there after a bit, Black Pawl said with the note of mockery in his voice:

"Good evening, Father!"

The missionary responded good-humoredly. He had been called harsher names in his time. Black Pawl leaned against the rail beside him. Beneath them, the water boiling about the *Deborah's* rudder glowed and sparkled and flamed in the bright moonlight, like silver fire. Deep below the surface a great fish darted diagonally past their stern and left a streak of flame to glow an instant, and die. The moon stitched every wave with a hem of mercury; and the valleys between the waves were blue as the heavens. The sea tossed in its sleep, about them. Black Pawl flung out his hand in a swift gesture, and said quietly:

"Looks dead, doesn't it! Yet there's not a drop of it but has its bit of life—from an eighty-foot cachalot to a spark of fire no bigger than a pin's point."

The missionary nodded. "The firmament showeth His handiwork," he quoted.

Black Pawl laughed. "Firmament? Maybe, Father. But that's land, not sea. I'm a man of the sea. Blame the works of the land on your God if you're a mind; but there's no God on deep waters."

The missionary glanced up with a quickened interest.

"You're of that belief, my friend?" he asked softly, nothing combative in his tone.

"Aye," replied Black Pawl. "There's never a God on the sea. That I know, having tried out the matter. And I even have my doubts about the land."

"What *is* your god?" asked the missionary.

"I have no God," answered Black Pawl; and his face was as his name.

The other shook his head. "Even a dog has his master for a god," he declared. "The god of some men is drink; of others, the flesh; of others, the work of their hands. But the god of wise men is—God." Looking steadily at Black Pawl, he asked again: "What *is* your god, my friend?"

The Captain laughed at that, stirring uneasily. "Spoken like a parson!" he retorted. "By their gods ye shall damn them: is that the idea?"

The missionary was silent for a little; then he smiled, and said: "I knew a man, once. He was an islander; and his god taught him to cut off the heads of his enemies, and cure them in smoke, and hang them up in his house. He was, I think, the finest man I ever knew—according to his lights. He had forty-two heads on the roof-tree of his hut; and I have no doubt—his own head was cut off finally—that he is clipping heads in paradise to-day."

"And if the elders of your church heard you say that, Father," Black Pawl told him, "they would cast you into outer darkness. Man, you were sent out here to tell the heathen they must love Christ or be damned. Were you not, now?"

"It was my friend's faith to cut off the heads of his enemies," said the missionary. "It is my faith to seek to show men the beauty of my faith. That is all the difference."

"Your God believes in advertising?"

"Yes," said the other; and he smiled again.

Black Pawl laughed. "That's worth hearing," he declared. "It's sense. Most of your cloth tell us to be humble, to be meek and lowly, like cattle. Why is goodness humble, Father? Why is virtue shy, and vice a braggart?"

"Just what do you mean, Cap'n Pawl?" the missionary asked. "I am interested."

"A man boasts of drink, of women, of a blow that is struck; but he does not boast of what you call a good deed. He advertises his crimes; he hides his virtues. Why?"

"Such a man does wrong," said the missionary. "He might better boast of his good deeds. Christ said: 'I am the son of God.' No mightier boast was ever uttered."

"Was it true?" Black Pawl asked, sharply.

"All men are God's sons—just as all men are God," the missionary explained.

The Captain nodded thoughtfully. "Then why not let it go at that?" he asked. "Why all this talk of heaven? Be good, and you will twingle the heavenly harps; be bad, and you will roast in hell. That's the way to convert a coward; but it's only a challenge to a strong man."

"Do you believe in the unpardonable sin?" the other countered.

Black Pawl's eyes clouded. "Yes," he confessed.

"Ah!" the missionary murmured half to himself. "I have been wondering why you were unhappy."

The Captain's face hardened at that. "The unhappy man is a coward," he parried.

"Then *you* are a coward, my friend."

"I am unhappy?"

"I think you are the most unhappy man I have ever known."

Black Pawl moved abruptly; he took six steps away and six steps back, then leaned against the rail again, unsmiling. And at last he lifted his head and dropped his hand on the missionary's shoulder. "Father," he said, "if your faith is worth anything, it must be practical. It must solve the problems of this world. Am I right?"

"Yes, my friend."

The captain of the *Deborah* nodded. "I am going to tell you a story of myself," he said. "Let your God write the answer to the riddle, if he can."

The missionary inclined his head. "Tell, if you wish to tell," he said.

"Listen, then," Black Pawl bade the missionary. 'You and I are poured in different molds, Father. But in one matter men are much alike. Did you ever love a woman?"

"Yes."

Black Pawl was gazing off across the purple night; it was almost as if the other were not there.

"I loved a woman," he went on. "I—loved

her. There was always an overflowing measure of life in me, perhaps. I poured it out on her. And she loved me as fully. She was tall and fair, and quiet as deep waters, Father. And she was very beautiful to look upon. Still — others thought her cold; she was not cold to me. There was a flame before us, and when we stepped into that flame hand in hand, we burned like welding metals. Burned, yet were not consumed! And we were welded like the metals, flesh and flesh, and soul and soul. We were no longer two people in those days; we were one. When others were about, we were like others, bantering, laughing, at ease—for each of us knew. But when we were alone, we were a living fire. Sometimes, seeing man and wife since then, I wonder if they are as we were. I wonder if behind the calm countenance of their open daily ife there is such a passionate devotion as that which welded us two.

"I say it welded us, Father. For by your God, she loved as much as I. She had a fashion of taking my cheeks in her hands, pinching them, pulling my face to meet hers, and shaking me to and fro as she did so. . . . Not even a woman could pretend like that. I say she loved me as I loved her.

"In the beginning, I say, this was so. She came one cruise with me, and the boy Red Pawl was born in a black storm not a hundred miles from here. I was doctor and nurse to her then, Father. She was brave. Aye! She lay in my arms throughout the torment, smiling up at me between the agonies. She was wiser than I in such matters, and she had brought a book that told what I must do, so that when the time came I was able to tend her—and the boy. I was clumsy; and I fumbled; but—the thing was done. It was a sacrament, Father. You see, I believed in your God in those days. It was a holy sacrament. I thought she was like your Christ, giving her flesh and her blood for this baby that was our world. She was holy to me. You say your faith is spiritual; but I say the true faith is physical. There is nothing so holy as the body, Father; for the holiest thing in the world is birth. If it were not holy, it would be unspeakably terrible. If there is a God, then the bringing of one body from another body is God's work, and man's work, and there is nothing so important in the world, and nothing so holy as this thing.

"The boy was born. We called him Dan. That is my name, you understand. But there cannot be two Dan Pawls; so he is *Red*, and I am *Black*, and there are few men whose memory runs to the contrary. He throve aboard the ship; and he was walking when we came home again.

"After that she would come no more to sea. She stayed at home next voyage, with the boy. And I tell you our love was as much a living thing while we were ten thousand miles apart as when we were each in the other's arms. And when I came home again, she was waiting for me.

"I was six months at home that time. The boy was past four when I came away; and his mother said he must come along and learn to know his father. To know me! So he came, and slept in my cabin, and learned the ship. He was stout for his age, even then; and before we turned for home that time, he was grown almost beyond his mother's knowledge. I told him: She will not know you.' And he laughed with me at that, and we planned to have him slip ashore and find her out, and fling himself upon her to see the tears of surprise that would spring into her eyes.

"All the long way home we planned that matter between us, you understand. And the boy's eyes would light, and my heart leaped to see him. And when the land lifted out of the sea ahead of us, we took our stand, we two, and watched for hours before we could sight the wharves where I told him she would be.

"I knew our coming would be signaled; she would know we were in the bay. So my glass searched the wharf, and the boy at my side clamored: 'Where is she, Daddy? Where is she, Daddy? Let me see.' And he took the glass from me and leveled it and looked. I could not tell him she was not there. So I pointed out a woman's figure, against a pile of oilbrown casks, and told him that was his mother. And he screamed his greeting to her across a solid mile of water. And I was straining my eyes for her coming along the wharf!"

For a moment Black Pawl paused. When he went on, there was no tremor in his voice. "We made fast," he said, "and still she had not come. And I saw by the way the others looked at me that something was amiss. I forgot the boy, in wondering; and I dared not question them, and the black fear shut down and clamped my heart. I forgot the boy; and before I knew, he was ashore, and had run to hug that woman I had shown him, and call her mother. And she put him away, and cried. So I thought my wife was dead.

"Even then I did not ask; and no one told me. I thought this was sympathy; I know, now, that it was because they were afraid. It was my brother who told me, in the end. He was not such a man as I am—smaller, and never overstrong. And when he told me, I struck him down, and he did not walk straight again during the two years more that he lived. Was that sin, that I did, in striking him?"

The pulse of the sea stirred the schooner's deck beneath them; their white wake foamed with silver fire. The moon moved serenely across the purple arch of the sky. The rigging overhead hummed beneath the thrumming fingers of the wind. The missionary looked out across the water, and then up into the eyes of Black Pawl, and beheld the deeps of agony there.

"Did your brother condemn you for that blow?" he asked gently.

"No."

"Then no man can do what he refused to do."

Black Pawl laughed sneeringly. "All right! Hear what he told me. Eight months after I was gone, our daughter was born to her. And six months after that, she and the child were away to sea with another man. Fleeing in the night secretly!"

He was still, on the word—still for so long that the missionary thought the story was ended. But before he could find words, the Captain spoke again.

"There is more," he said. "Will you hear it?"

"Yes."

"We got away quickly on another cruise, my son and I. And another after that, and another. And after the third returning, they told me at home that the man with whom she had fled had come back alone. He said she had left him as she had left me. He was gone before I returned. But I knew that some day I would come upon him.

"Red Pawl was full-grown by then—big for his years. He was cabin-boy, one cruise; and fourth mate on the next; and mate the cruise after. It was his first cruise as mate that we found the man."

There was a cold intensity in Black Pawl's tone, and he asked again as if in challenge: "Will you hear?"

"Yes."

"Ill luck had pursued that man," Black Pawl went on evenly now. "They said his ship was a death-ship. Men died easily upon it; and it was hard for that vessel to find whales. Also it was hard for him to persuade men to ship with him. His officers were unlucky; and to be unlucky in the whale-fisheries is to die. He was driven to fight the whales himself. And it was thus, in the end, that he came into my hands.

My son's boat picked him up one day. He had lowered for a whale, and got fast; and the fish ran with him till he was lost from his ship; and then he was forced to cut. Thereafter thirst fell upon that boat. Because he was strong, and because that was the breed of the man, he kept more than his fair measure of the water in the lantern-keg. So when Red Pawl found him drifting under the sun, only this man was left alive in the boat. There was another, dead, with him —his boat-steerer. He had thrown the others overside.

"The man was insane with thirst when Red found him. But he wouldn't have known the boy, in any case; and Red didn't know him. He brought him back to the schooner; and we took him into my cabin to nurse him back to life, and I knew him—there.

"When he was sane, he knew me; but he said nothing, hoping I did not know. And I said nothing until he was himself again, strong and well. In due time, one day, he wished to leave the cabin and go on deck. So I knew it was time for that which I meant to do.

"We tied this man, my son and I. We tied him in the bunk, and gagged him. I had told Red who he was, and Red wanted to slit his throat; but I would not do that. Red lacks imagination. I told him so.

"We tied him in his bunk, and gagged him. I told him then that I knew him; and I told him what I meant to do. It was in my mind to let him lie there without food or water till he died before my eyes. I believed then, and I still believe, that to do this would have been to show too much mercy.

"But when I told him what I meant to do, he made signs that he wished to speak; and I took away the gag from his mouth. He was a man of a certain rat-like courage, Father. He taunted me to my teeth; and he told me, among other things, that when he was tired of the woman I had loved, he had given her into the hands of an evil crew I knew of, and the child with her, and he said they had died unspeakably.

"That he spoke truth was plain in the man's eye. I knew why he told me. It was to move me to give him the mercy of quick death; but I would not. Then he called me coward, and said that I would not face him as a man. So I laughed and told him he should have his wish to face me. He said he was weak. That was true. And I was hungry to feel his strong flesh break in my hands. I considered what we might do.

"What we did was this, Father: I turned the schooner toward an island of which I knew—a place where no humans lived. There we stayed a length of time, till the man was well; and there, when the time was ripe, we fought.

"I killed him. He was stronger than I; and he battered me badly before I could close with him. Then I broke his right arm between my hands, so that he screamed; and after that I beat him with my fists, and when he fell, Red Pawl lifted him, and held him, and I beat him to death with my bare hands. The fight lasted from morning until halfway to noon. It was a good fight until I broke his arm; after that— He died on his feet, Red Pawl's arms supporting him. And when he was dead, we left him there; and when the schooner made out of that anchorage, sir, the birds were already a heap of white upon him, where he lay."

Black Pawl stopped, with that; and for a long time neither man spoke. At last, uneasy at the silence, Black Pawl laughed to hide his unrest.

"So, Father," he said at last, "what has your God to say to that?"

"Have you ever found trace of your wife, Black Pawl?" the missionary asked.

"I found those men to whom he gave her. They denied the tale. But Red Pawl and I killed three of them, and broke the other two."

The missionary made no comment; and Black Pawl asked again: "What will your God say to that, Father?"

Then the man of the church looked up at the other and said gently: "I am sorry for you, Dan Pawl."

The Captain sneered. "Don't waste sorrow on me. I've no regrets."

"It is not because of the past that I am sorry for you," replied the missionary. "It is because of that which must surely come."

CHAPTER IV.

THERE developed in Black Pawl a devil of unrest. It is in all men; it was stronger in him, just as every function of the man was stronger than a like function in other men. Beneath his mirthless laughter, beneath his malign joviality, there was a hatred of the world, a hatred which could not find expression.

It showed itself, curiously, in his attitude toward the crew. His fists were ever ready; they struck more and more frequently as the days passed. Yet when he struck, the man always laughed. It was as if his laughter were the curb he put upon himself. It was possible to imagine that if he had not laughed, his least impatience would become a murderous rage. He might have killed for small offenses; but he laughed, and so refrained.

His men, for the most part, felt this without understanding it. There was always a strange loyalty in Black Pawl's crews; this was well known, and it puzzled those who knew. There were more blows struck on his ship than on any other that pretended to decency; yet the crew were loyal. Ashore they were ever ready to fight to defend him. They had, in some sort, a love for him. They felt, without understanding why, a sympathy for the man. Once one of the older men, who had sailed with him four full cruises, put this into words.

"He means naught," this man said. "The fist is a fashion of speech with him. The man is torn, and weary o' the world. That's easy seen. There's a load on him."

So they took his buffets, and picked themselves up, and grinned good-naturedly, and would not take offense.

There were, on the *Deborah*, but two exceptions to this rule. One was Red Pawl, his son and mate. When Red Pawl struck a man, there was murder in the blow and poison in the eye that guided it.

Shunned by every man, and hating every man, he had no friend aboard. He was like a mad dog in one thing; his deeper hatred was directed toward his master, his father, the one man he should have loved and served. Just as a dog that is mad will bite first the best-loved hand, just as an elephant upon whom madness comes will trample first his own *mahout,* in like fashion Red Pawl's hatred centered on his father. It was this hatred which gave the impulse to his efforts to cultivate the crew, to breed discontent and to bring matters to a point that would end in the Captain's destruction.

He had, it is true, little success; nevertheless he persisted. The one man aboard who listened to him willingly was Spiess, him whom Black Pawl had struck that day they took the missionary and the girl aboard. This Spiess was, aside from Red Pawl, the only man aboard who had not a secret sympathy for the tragedy plain upon the Captain's face. He hated Black Pawl with the hatred of the weak for the strong; and the Captain saw this, and took a mocking delight in nagging Spiess, and bullying him, and driving him toward the point of open strife.

This was near, one day, when Black Pawl stepped down from the quarter and started toward the waist of the schooner. Spiess was on his knees, scrubbing the deck. The Captain, as he passed, kicked out at the man, and Spiess was tumbled forward on his face, while Black Pawl laughed. "Keep out o' the path, Spiess," the Captain warned him.

Spiess got up lumberingly, and looked around. Red Pawl was on the quarter, and Spiess caught his eye. Beyond Red were Dan Darrin and the girl. These two were much together as time passed; but Spiess saw only Red Pawl, and read, perhaps, encouragement in his eye. For he turned and rushed the Captain with the blind ferocity of a bull.

Black Pawl's face set grimly as the man charged; and he met Spiess with an open-handed blow on one cheek, and then on the other, that brought the seaman up all standing and trembling with the dizzy nausea the jarring blows induced. While he stood thus, helpless, Black Pawl struck out like the kick of a mule and Spiess went spinning and teetering across the deck till he came to the opposite rail, where he collapsed.

As Spiess lifted his head, Black Pawl laughed and said: "Bring better than your fists, next time, Spiess."

The man muttered under his breath: "Aye, I will." And Black Pawl nodded cheerfully, and forgot his errand in the waist and returned to the quarter again. There Red Pawl, openly rebellious, warned him:

"I tell you, keep your hands off the men of my boat, sir."

"Fiddle!" grinned his father. "Teach your men manners, boy." And he passed Red and joined the girl. She had watched, she was watching now, with a white, still face. Black Pawl felt a curious necessity of apologizing to her for what he had done. But he did not; for it was not the nature of the man. He challenged her instead. "One way of handling that like of man, Ruth," he said.

She replied boldly: "A bad way, Cap'n Pawl."

He laughed at that, and touched her under the chin, lightly. "Now, now! It serves."

She felt that she ought to condemn him, but she could not. The spell of the man was upon her, as it was upon the others. She liked him, could not forbear liking him, no matter what he might do. There was charm in him; and there was, for all his strength and pride of strength, a weakness that appealed to the mother heart of her. She was sorry for him, without knowing why. Indeed she did not even know she was sorry for him; she only knew she liked him, whatever he might do. So in spite of herself she found she must smile at him now. He said, catching the smile: "So, that's better."

"You'll find the men don't mind," Dan Darrin had told her one day. "They take it as a part of the game; and there never was a crew that would stick closer in trouble."

She nodded, and murmured thoughtfully: "I can believe that men would stick with you."

He looked forward along the length of his ship, an uninvited wistfulness in eye and curve of lip. "Aye, Ruth, they do," he said. Then, with his mirthless laugh, he added: "Lord knows why!"

She wondered, when she was alone, why she felt so drawn to the man. He personified, she thought, those brutalities which she should condemn; yet she liked him, admired him—and something more. There was a tenderness in her for Black Pawl that she could neither define nor deny. It increased her wonder, even frightened her a little. She told the old missionary of this; and he explained:

"There's fundamental good in him; that is all. In spite of himself, Black Pawl is a fine, good man."

When she and Darrin were together, she made him tell her about Black Pawl; and nothing more delighted Darrin. For he loved Black Pawl; and the man he painted for the girl was of heroic proportions and Viking strength, and the stories he told of his exploits were like legends. Ruth asked him, one day, what Black Pawl's name had been, and Dan told her. "He was christened *Dan*; and his son too," he said.

She smiled with surprise. "Three of you *Dans* about the *Deborah*; and all officers!" Her eyes clouded thoughtfully, and she fell silent. She remembered a thing her mother had once said to her. "Trust a man named *Dan*," her mother had said. "They're good men, Ruth. It goes with the name."

She had wondered, then, whether her father had been named *Dan*, and asked her mother. The woman shivered faintly, and said: "No; *Michael* he was—*Michael Lytton,* Ruth. Never forget that name."

Her mother had told her very little about this man who had been her father. He had died, she said, when Ruth was still a baby. Thought of him came to her now; then she put the thought aside and fell to talking to Dan Darrin again, and their talk ran on and on.

"Trust a man named *Dan,*" her mother had said; and she had trusted and liked Dan Darrin from the beginning. She was a girl; a girl's fancies run very tenderly on such things as names.

Yet she had not at all the same feeling toward Red Pawl, even though his name were also *Dan.* She disliked him; and his insistent companionship annoyed her. Sometimes she was hard put to be rid of him.

Black Pawl perceived this, one morning when she turned away from the mate with hot cheeks and hurried below; and his eyes, as he looked on his son thereafter, were lowering.

But Red Pawl did not see. He was looking toward the cabin companion, down which the girl had disappeared.

CHAPTER V

THE grim story which the missionary had heard from Black Pawl stayed in his mind; he could not put it aside. He thought upon it constantly, wondering, seeking, puzzling for the key.

He hesitated to speak of it again to Black Pawl. Since that night of confidences the Captain had avoided him, with something shamefaced in his manner, as if he regretted having spoken. The man of the church was not one to harass another; he knew Black Pawl must hate to think or speak of that which had passed. But the missionary's mind dwelt on it constantly; he watched Black Pawl, and pondered.

There is a certain comfort and solace in talking of our own miseries. It is as though, by revealing them to others, we shift the burden of the load from our own shoulders. Black Pawl, until he spoke to the missionary, had never tasted this measure of comfort; and having tasted, it was inevitable, finally, that he should seek it again. The missionary understood this, as he considered the matter; and so he waited with some patience, and in the end, as he expected, Black Pawl brought up the tale once more.

"I've been wondering, Father," he said with a mockery of respect in his tones, "just what you meant by saying you pitied me for what must surely come."

The missionary did not answer at once; and when he did, it was with another question. "Black Pawl," he said, "are you sure your wife and your child are dead?"

The Captain laughed bitterly. "Sure."

"You told me the — evil men — denied the thing."

"At first, yes," said Black Pawl. "But at the last, just before I broke his neck, seeking to save the worthless life in him, the chief of them admitted the whole."

The missionary considered, eyes afar with his thoughts. "Was there any way," he asked, "by which you might have known them, if you had ever found the two? Not your wife only, but — your daughter."

"Aye," said Black Pawl. "I would know." His voice was dead in his throat.

"But you never saw the child."

"No."

"How could you know?"

The Captain flung about, and asked harshly: "Should I not know my own?"

There was a gentle persistence in the missionary. He ignored the rebuff. "Cap'n Pawl," he said, "there are strange chances in this world. It is impossible ever to be *sure*."

"It is *not* impossible," said the Captain. "For I *am* sure."

"That dying man may have lied."

Black Pawl threw back his head. "Father," he said, "I thought of that. I called him a liar. And he showed me a drawer hidden in the cabin of their filthy schooner; and from the drawer he picked out for me a wedding-ring. I knew it. So was I sure."

"So—the wedding-ring." It was as though the missionary spoke to himself; then he asked: "Have you the ring?"

"Aye," answered Black Pawl.

The man of the church considered a moment.

"You gave her other—jewels, I have no doubt," he suggested. "Did this man have them as well?"

Black Pawl shook his head. "She was not one for such baubles. There was only a little locket. When I left her, at the last, with our son, we made a daguerreotype of him, that she might wear it in this locket about her throat. It was not worth the stealing, or it was lost before the end. At least, this man had it not."

"You asked him for it?"

"No. When he showed me the wedding-ring, he was in five seconds of death."

"What was that locket like?" the missionary pursued.

But Black Pawl could endure no more. "Man," he cried, "have done!" His voice broke with a laugh. "This digging in dead years is fool's work, Father," he said. "Have done with it, for good and all."

For a space of minutes the missionary stood musing, while Black Pawl paced the deck behind him, now and again roaring orders to laggers amidships. In the end he paused, then drew near the missionary again.

"Why do you pity me, Father?" he asked. "You've not told that."

The calm eyes looked up at him; and the man of the church answered steadily: "Because of the thing that is before you, Cap'n Pawl."

Black Pawl laughed. "Aye, you said that. Prophesy, Father — prophesy! What *is* before me?"

"You love your son?" asked the missionary. Black Pawl's face twisted, and he laughed again.

"Oh, aye!" he said.

"Because he *is* your son, blood of your blood," the man of the church defined. "But— you also hate your son."

The Captain was smiling grimly. "Have it so. This is paradox, not prophecy."

"There is evil in him," said the missionary. "The blood that you gave him, the life you have shown him—these have bred evil in the man. And you have justice in you; and because of that justice, you hate the evil in Red Pawl. I pity you, Captain, because some day you must choose between the blood-son whom you love and the evil son whom you hate. And that will not be an easy choice."

Black Pawl snapped his fingers. "Fiddle!" he exclaimed. "I've laid hands on him as a boy; I can do it still. I can chastise, if there's need."

"Red Pawl is no longer a boy," replied the missionary. "He is *the worst of you*, alive before your eyes, my friend."

"Well?" the Captain challenged. "Is it not something to see your sins so plainly?"

The missionary hesitated; then he held out his hand and smiled. "Captain," he said, "you are a man, and my friend. Whether you believe in their worth or no, you have my prayers."

"They'll do no harm, at the least," answered Black Pawl; and a simple and honest gratitude for this friendship was behind the mockery in his tones.

CHAPTER VI

ON the second day afterward, the *Deborah* ran into the fringes of bad weather. In mid-morning the wind began to rise unpleasantly; the glass was falling, and the skies were overcast. Black Pawl had been driving the schooner under full canvas. He was a bold man without being a reckless one, and when the signs turned against him, he ordered topsails furled and reefs in fore and main. It was Dan Darrin's watch on deck, and Dan went forward to direct the work. Black Pawl was aft, with the old missionary. The mate was below in his cabin, Ruth in hers.

When the work was under way, the Captain turned and said: "Best come below, Father. This wind's a rough one."

The old missionary shook his head. His cheeks were ruddy with the buffets of wind and spray, and his eyes were shining. "There's still sap enough in this old body of mine to like it," he said.

Black Pawl laughed. Then he caught Dan Darrin's eye and bade him watch for a space. He meant to go below for his storm gear and return to take the deck. It was in his mind to be no more than a minute below; but when he dropped down the companion, the ship, and the brewing storm and the sea were all forgotten in what he beheld.

The door of the girl's cabin was open. Beyond this open doorway Ruth was struggling in the arms of Red Pawl. She was fighting silently, pushing at him with her hands against his breast. And Red was laughing, and whispering to her.

At the sight Black Pawl felt something surge in his breast that he had not known was there, a hot flood of passion and anger. For an instant he stood quite still, choking against the beating of his own heart; and his face turned black. The girl saw him, and called softly across the cabin:

"Cap'n Pawl—please."

He had time to mark, even then, that her voice was level and unafraid.

As she spoke, Red Pawl turned his head, and

over his shoulder beheld his father. He loosed the girl, and turned, half crouching. He moved forward two steps, to the cabin table, and rested his great hands on it, and gazed at Black Pawl eye to eye.

That instant the flood of passion in the Captain's heart burst its bounds. He leaped forward with the swift and silent ferocity of a beast; and at sight of his convulsed face, the girl shuddered. But she held her ground in the corner, watching. The cabin was so small that there was no room for any maneuvering; the table in the center left only narrow ways about the sides. It was like witnessing the battle of two lions in a pit.

Black Pawl, in his charge, seemed not to see the table. He struck it with his thighs; and stout as it was, and secure as it was in its place upon the floor, it was wrenched loose and flung against Red Pawl, bearing him back; and for an instant he was pinned against the wall, the table against his legs, his father's huge knotted fists lashing at him.

Since Red was a child, Black Pawl had never struck him in anger. And now, at those first blows, the son was whipped to a fury as fierce as that of Black Pawl. He ducked, bent his back, and thrust the table from his knees; he came on Black Pawl then, from the side, head down. He got his arms about the other's middle; their two bodies crashed down upon the table, smashing it to splinters.

The sudden tumult in the cabin had brought the missionary and Dan Darrin, running. Pinned in his son's arms, Black Pawl saw them, and he called in stern, sure tones:

"Dan, on deck! Take the ship. Father, stand away. I've a lesson to teach here."

Dan obeyed instantly; the missionary paused by the companion, watching. Tighter Red Pawl's arms wound about his father, as though he would crush the older man.

Red was the stronger. He was built broad, built thick, built solid upon the ground, whereas Black Pawl was lean and long. Nevertheless, Black Pawl had more of the lore of rough and tumble; and through the years his strength had ripened, not decayed. Held down now by the heavier man, crushed in that viselike grip, he cooled to a deadly ferocity; then worked his long arm up for a blow that, when it fell, rocked

Red's head upon his shoulders. For an instant only the other's muscles slacked, but the instant was enough to let Black Pawl get his elbow beneath the other's throat, and thrust up and away. Red was finally forced to yield, for if he had not, his head must have been torn from his shoulders. He writhed back, shifting to obtain a fresh hold, and Black Pawl squirmed to one side, and to his feet, and so was free. He stepped back, breathing deep into his strangled lungs; instantly Red sprang to his feet, lowered his head and charged.

Black Pawl was too wise to send home a blow a-top that lowered head. He had seen many an unwise man break a fist thus and lose thereby. As Red came near, he stepped to one side with a lagging foot, and Red stumbled over this foot, and went into the cabin wall with a crash that would have stunned a weaker man. As he straightened, Black Pawl met him with a blow full in the face that drove Red's head back against the paneling. Then the younger man ducked, and blocked with cunning elbows and shoulders hunched high, and strove again to come to closer quarters.

Black Pawl was still too nimble for him. It was like a bullfight. Red was the bull, and Black Pawl's blows pricked him again and again as he charged fruitlessly upon and past the older man. In the end, Red understood that what he wished to do could not be done in this way; he must stand and fight. And so he changed his tactics. Standing back, he took his ease and caught his breath while Black Pawl pushed the fighting. Red was content to guard, take what blows came, and wait till his strength was restored again.

When he was ready, he lifted his head and began.

In such fighting as this, Black Pawl had all the advantage; he was taller, and swifter of foot, and he had three inches the reach of the other man. His knuckles cut Red's cheek, smashed Red's mouth, beat a tattoo upon his face that would have killed another man. As for Red, he did not strike for the head. He was plugging at Black Pawl's ribs, but Black Pawl's fists had a way of tapping Red's biceps or wrists in a fashion that took the strength from these blows. Meanwhile, he landed almost at will upon his son; and any one of a dozen blows he struck would have plunged a weaker man swiftly into oblivion.

After a time this became plain to both of them. Red realized that Black Pawl could not hurt him, that he could endure the worst the older man could send; and Black Pawl knew this as quickly as his son. Nevertheless, he would cut Red to pieces with his blows. The mate must weaken in the end. He struck, and struck, and struck again.

Red lowered his head into the shelter of his left shoulder and rested his right arm, fending with the left. And he began to wait, and wait, and watch for the chance he sought. Soon or late, his father's chin must come within reach of that waiting fist. And when it did—

His chance came quickly. He ducked a straightforward blow that slid across his shoulder, and brought Black Pawl's face within a few inches of his own. Before the Captain could guard, Red's right whipped up squarely on the chin, a little to the left of the point, where the full jolt of it was instantly communicated through jawbone and skull to those nerves which bear to the muscles the messages of the brain.

Black Pawl went spinning backward, slack and weak and helpless; and Red gathered his breath and leaped.

There was no more than a second's space between Red's blow and his charge, but that second was long enough for the sickness to pass —long enough for Black Pawl to gain control of his shaking body once more. Then Red had him around the waist again; he felt his son's hip thrust against his thigh and knew what was coming—the throw for which there is no guard, no defense except to yield to it. Black Pawl let himself go limply, but as his feet left the floor, his hands reached out and got the grip he sought. His long fingers closed on his son's neck. He sank them home, pressing—pressing.

He was in the air, all his weight flying. Yet his hands still gripped the other's throat. So the momentum of his own throw dragged Red Pawl forward, overbalancing him. He fell a-top Black Pawl in a rolling heap, and Black Pawl's thumbs sank in between the great muscles at the side of the neck, and the gullet in front. Their paralyzing pressure stopped Red's breath, stopped the blood in the great arteries that feed the brain. He felt insensibility enveloping him; then with a mighty effort he flung his elbow into Black Pawl's throat and broke the hold. For an instant again he was free of that choking terror. They were grappling, entwined like snakes in a knot upon the floor.

Black Pawl's hand slid beneath his son's arm; and with all his strength he drove his thumb in against the tender flesh that covers the ribs at the armpit. There is no more excruciating pain; Red Pawl screamed with it, and fumbled frantically for his father's wrist.

Instantly Black Pawl's fingers found the other's throat again; Red slackened and choked, and was limp. Black Pawl shook him, once, and twice; and then he flung him to one side, and rose upright, and stood gazing down upon his prostrate son.

His shirt was torn away; his iron-gray hair was down about his eyes. Blood smeared his shoulder and his mouth. Still he was an heroic and unconquerable figure, strong and sure. The girl who had watched it all in silence from the doorway now uttered a soft, almost breathless cry. Black Pawl looked toward her, and laughed through his bloody lips, and then looked down again upon his son, who was choking back to life. The missionary had stood impassive by the companion throughout the fight, watching the two men.

All three now watched the man on the floor. Red Pawl groaned and gasped, and so at last could breathe again. He sat up weakly, supporting himself on his arm. Black Pawl bent and lifted him with a hand upon his collar; he slapped Red harshly on the cheek. .

"On deck!" he said. "On deck with you. And sharp, now!"

With one murderous look at his father, Red Pawl turned and staggered to the companion. Halfway up, he paused and looked again at the Captain through level eyes. Black Pawl laughed and waved a careless hand. "Sharp, there!" he said.

Red went up to the deck, disappearing from their sight. When he was gone, his father glanced uncertainly around and began to tremble and sway upon his feet. Then he sank softly to the floor, and leaning heavily against the cabin wall, he closed his eyes.

The girl came running to him, sobbing; and when he opened his eyes and saw her face bent above him, he smiled; the old mockery danced in his eyes, and he flung an arm about her neck and drew her down and kissed her, still laughing.

"I've earned that, haven't I?" he challenged.

She crimsoned and into her eyes flashed a look of hurt and sorrow. The old missionary turned from one to the other, but said nothing.

"Come, you don't grudge that kiss?" Black Pawl demanded of her gayly.

She answered quietly: "I'd have—given it. I'm sorry that you took it so."

"Then give it," the Captain bade her.

And she bent and kissed him on the forehead, her hand upon his hair. And the heart in his bosom leaped at the caress.

"Was not that a fight worth seeing, Ruth?" he cried. "Worth winning?"

"It was terrible," she told him. "Oh, even though he is your son, I'm afraid for you. There was death in his eyes, Cap'n Pawl."

At that the Captain laughed again, and stumbling to his feet, stood swaying above them.

"Fiddle!" he said. "He's fanciful. But he's not a man to fear, not Red Pawl."

The girl looked at the missionary, and saw her own fear mirrored in his eyes, and something of sorrow as well. But she said no more.

CHAPTER VII

AFTER the fight with his son, a change came over Cap'n Pawl, a change which made the missionary uneasy.

Black Pawl said to him next day: "Well, Father, you were a true prophet. The thing came about as you said. But you see, it is finished, with no harm done after all."

"It has come," said the missionary. "But it is not finished."

"You're a persistent prophet, at least," the Captain answered. "What more will there be?"

The other replied: "Have you marked the mate's fashion of whispering among the crew?"

"Yes; Red was always a whisperer."

"Is there no harm to be foreseen in that?"

Black Pawl chuckled and waved his hand. "I'm harsh with my men, but they love me," he boasted. "They even tell me what Red whispers to them. Not one would listen to him."

"Not one?" the missionary asked; and Black Pawl said again:

"Not one."

He spoke surely. But there was doubt in him; there was a dreadful doubt which he would not admit, but could not down. He had seen, as well as any man, the blackness of Red's heart in the man's eye after their conflict. He had seen the evil in the man; and because Red was his son, and because Red was evil, Black Pawl's heart was near the breaking-point.

He hid this, or sought to hide it, as he was accustomed to hide all the tragedy in his life. He became more boisterous, more bold, more given to the mockery of his laughter. A devil of recklessness came to life in him. The native decency of him was drowned in the agony of Red's self-betrayal. Red was his son, his only blood in all the world; and if Red Pawl were worthless, what was there left in life? What use in righteousness?

Hand in hand with this recklessness of despair, there was another and uglier impulse stirring in him. There had never been for him but one woman; there never could be another, he told himself, whom he would not scorn. And yet—he could not scorn Ruth Lytton.

There was tenderness in him for her; and because he had always told himself he could never harbor tenderness for any woman, he would not accept this feeling for what it was. He respected her, yet told himself that no woman deserved respect, since the one woman had proved lacking. He liked Ruth; yet he swore that no woman was worth liking, since one had been false. Yet a tender affection for Ruth grew in him, persisted. Since it was neither liking nor love, what could it be? He knew, and laughed, scorning himself, and her, and all the world.

But in the days that followed the fight, his thoughts came back and beat and beat again along this groove. And he watched her, wondering, wondering. The thought of her tormented him. That she was fair and clean and fine was torture to him who believed none fair nor clean nor fine. Unconsciously, he matched her against Red Pawl, his son; and because she was good where Red was evil, he thought he hated her.

Yet he had fought for her—yes, and won for her. He laughed unpleasantly at the thought. He remembered her kiss upon his forehead, and the touch of her gentle hand upon his hair, and his heart ached at the memory. When he thought of that other kiss which he had taken from her, he was revolted. Yet he had taken such kisses before, and never loathed himself for them. Since she was so fair, why was she not fit for such kisses as other women gave? Why were her lips softly upon his forehead sweeter than her lips against his own?

He flung the mystery aside. Forget! Not worth the wondering! But he could not forget.

Black Pawl was more unhappy in these days than he had ever been before. For he knew now, more surely than ever, how much he loved Red Pawl. His son and hers, son of the one woman he had loved. His memories lingered about the baby that had first come to sea with him; and he contemplated the manhood to which that baby had come, and his heart ached. Alone, his head bowed upon his arms. There were times when he longed to go to the missionary for aid and counsel; but he put the wish away. This was a load that he alone must bear. Whatever his son was, he, Black Pawl, had made him so.

He wanted, desperately, at first, to go to the boy and wipe the strife away; he wanted to make up with his son. His memory went back to the days of comradeship when Red was still a lad, and he was sick with longing for their return. He thought of the black chapters of the life he had led his son; and he lashed his own soul with the whips of memory. He tried, once, on the second day, to speak to Red as though nothing were amiss between them; but the mate gave him a level stare from dark and lowering eyes, and Black Pawl turned away. No words had passed between them since their battle. Black Pawl knew in his heart that no words of the old comradely sort would ever pass between them again.

He accepted this, at last, with the old reckless laugh. There was whisky in a bottle in his cabin. He drank deep of it.

It was not like Black Pawl to surrender to man or God; but in these days he was near surrender. He drank with a certain regularity, as the days passed. He was never fuddled; his eye was never clouded. But he was never quite sober; there was always a reckless bravado, an unreasoning and unreckoning carelessness about him.

On deck, one day, Black Pawl talked with Ruth

Lytton. The girl had sensed something of the sorrow and misery that enveloped him. She was drawn to him by a sympathy which was stronger than she knew. She pitied him profoundly, and would have helped him, and tried, in unostentatious ways, to cheer and comfort him; and when she knew there was liquor in him, she was sorry and uneasy.

He asked her this day how she liked the voyage. She told him she was happy. This was not true. She was too sorry for him to be happy. He reminded her of the stiff gale they had fought, at the time of his battle with his son. "Were you frightened?" he asked.

She shook her head. "No," she said. "I was not afraid."

He touched her hand suddenly, and held it, chuckling. "You're a pretty nervy thing, for a woman, seems to me."

"I am not often afraid," she said.

He caught her shoulder and turned her toward him then. "Ever afraid of me?" he asked.

She smiled. "No."

"Not even when I grabbed that kiss—in the cabin?"

"No, I could never be afraid of you," she told him, eyes meeting his bravely.

Dan Darrin came just then, with a question, and while he and the Captain spoke together, the girl moved away and went below. Black Pawl, watching her, scarce heard what Darrin was saying. Damn the girl, so clean and brave and good! She'd best be afraid of him. He thought he might teach her that trick, some day.

When Dan was gone, he cursed himself for a black dog because of his thought. But—the drink was in him, and his heart was sick for Red Pawl, and there was nothing in the world ahead.

CHAPTER VIII

WHEN Black Pawl boasted to the missionary that the men forward were so loyal they brought him word of Red Pawl's talk to them, he spoke the truth. When he said there was not one of them who listened to the mate, he was mistaken. There was one — Spiess. Spiess had always received more than his share of rough usage; the man was a natural target for harsh words and for blows. Furthermore, he had not that fundamental good nature which made the others of the crew laugh at Black Pawl's cheerful buffets. Also he lacked that sympathy of heart which dwelt in the others, and let them see the despair which the Captain hid behind his amiable violence.

Spiess listened to Red Pawl, and listened assentingly. Red made a dupe of the man, using him for his own ends. The mate hated his father; also he feared him. He called down death, in his thoughts, upon the Captain's head;

but he would never have dared strike the blow himself. He might have done it, a dozen times. Black Pawl was careless of his own safety. He never wore about him one of the revolvers which were kept in the cabin. Darrin was like him in this; but Red Pawl habitually went armed. The Captain trusted to his fists, and with some reason. He was the match of any two men aboard, saving perhaps his son, in using those lean fists of his.

Red Pawl told Spiess this, one day. "You talk and curse at him, under your breath," the mate said openly to the other. "But what good is that? He masters you with his open hands. You can never touch him with them. Remember, he told you to bring better than fists next time."

And Spiess, gripping the wheel-spokes, said under his breath: "Aye; and I will."

Red Pawl laughed. "You will—thus; and you will—so," he derided. "But you do—nothing, save take what he gives, and mouth at him behind his back."

"I will," Spiess told him. And he glanced at the mate sidewise. "When I do, like is, you'll be on my back."

Red Pawl was past caution by this time, in his hatred of the Captain. "When you do," he said, "I'll be left master o' the *Deborah*. I'll be *at* your back, not *on* it. And—I'll see the log is entered in a fashion you'd like. *When* you do!"

Spiess looked at him suspiciously. He was not a trusting man. "When I do," he said sullenly, "you can log and be damned."

Then Black Pawl came up from below, and Red moved away from the wheel, and the Captain laughed at them both.

That boast of Black Pawl's—that his men told him Red Pawl's whisperings—was in his mind next day when old Flexer, who had sailed twelve years in Black Pawl's ships, came to him. Flexer had been boat-steerer, and by the same token harpooner, in the boat of the lost third mate whose place had never been filled. He lived with the other harpooners just forward of the cabin. He and his fellows were neither flesh nor fowl—they were not of the crew; they were not of the cabin. Theirs was an intermediate status, and they had privileges. The crew, for example, never came aft of the try-works except upon duties assigned them; but the harpooners were free of the schooner from knight's-heads to galley, just at the break of deck. There were three of them; one was an islander, and one was of Cape Verde. Flexer, of New England stock, kept himself somewhat aloof from the other two. Also, he had his cronies forward.

He found an opportunity, one day when Red Pawl was below, to speak with the Captain; and he wasted no words in the matter. "Black Pawl," he said in the tone of an old friend rather than that of an underling, "you're a bold man; and there's boldness in me too. I'm minded to tell you a thing that will bring your anger on me."

Black Pawl looked at the other with narrowed eyes; then he chuckled, and warned the man: "Best look sharp. I'm like to knock you the deck's length if I'm displeased with you. I'm a harsh man with my fists, Flexer."

"Aye," said Flexer gently. "But—not harsh in your heart, sir."

Black Pawl looked astonished. "You've marked that?" he mocked.

Flexer said stubbornly: "You mark this, sir. The mate means harm to you."

The Captain's face set for a moment; then he said cheerfully: "So I guessed, in the cabin t'other day, when he tried to crush my in'ards in his arms."

"Aye, I've heard of that," Flexer said. "But—that was honest fighting, fists and feet. I'm meaning worse."

For a moment he thought Black Pawl would strike; and he guessed there was liquor in the Captain. But the master of the ship held his hand. "What worse are you meaning, Flexer?" he asked.

"This," said Flexer: "that if the fools for'ard believed half he whispered to them, there'd be a knife in your back in an hour."

Black Pawl laughed aloud. "Fiddle, man!" he cried. "I've had knives in every inch of me, back and front. They no more than let a little blood."

"Red Pawl would rather they let out a little life," said Flexer.

Black Pawl flung the warning aside. "Even Red can't always have his d'ruthers," he replied.

"There is the minister," Flexer urged. "And

—there is the girl. They shipped with you, on your ship—not Red Pawl's. And even if they had not, even if they were strangers ashore, even then, Black Pawl, it would be for you to guard against this son of yours."

"Did I not curb him in the cabin?"

"I tell you no. I tell you there is death in his eye, for you; and worse for them."

"For her?"

"For her."

Black Pawl twisted away. "And why not?" he demanded. "Why is she better than another woman, to be so guarded? Let her take life, rough as it comes, as others do."

Flexer looked in his captain's eye; and there was flat condemnation in his gaze. Before his eyes the Captain's fell.

"Old wives' tales, Flexer," he said mockingly. "Forget them; and be still, man—be still."

CHAPTER IX

RUTH LYTTON was sick with unhappiness for the sake of Black Pawl. She was sorry for him because his son was false; she was sorrier for him because Black Pawl was false to himself. He was drinking more and more; there was an ugly note in his voice, and an ugly devil in his eye. If she could have hated him, she would not have been unhappy; but since in spite of herself she had a tender liking for the man, she was miserable.

She found her only release from this unhappiness in the occasional hours she spent with Dan Darrin; yet she did not at first understand the significance of this. Love needs to be recognized. His counterfeit is never modest, never hidden; but love may slumber, and love may hide. Ruth Lytton's discovery of the fact that she loved Dan Darrin came about quite simply, in this fashion:

It was in the late afternoon; she and Dan were

together on the quarter. The wind had fallen at noon; it was so near a flat and dead calm that the schooner's sails were not drawing. The sun was going down in a blaze of crimson, hot and still. Dan had sent men aloft to tar the rigging here and there; and one of these men was working on the main yard, above the quarter where they stood. Dan and the girl had been talking about the weather. It did not matter what they talked about, what words they spoke. They had come to that point where even silence is a rich communion. Nevertheless, it chanced they were talking about the weather, and specifically, about the approaching sunset.

Then the man on the yard, high above them, had occasion to shift his tar-pot; and in the shifting let it slip and fall. He bellowed down his warning: " 'Ware below." Ruth looked up swiftly and saw the heavy bucket falling.

According to the laws of physics, a falling object drops sixteen feet in one second, sixty-four in two—in a vacuum. The man on the yard was perhaps forty, perhaps fifty feet above the deck. So, even allowing for the resistance of the still, hot air, it was no more than two seconds between the time the bucket started to fall and the time it would reach the deck. Nevertheless that space of time was for Ruth Lytton as long as eternity. She looked up at the man's cry, and saw the bucket half way down, descending with a ponderous and deadly majesty, slowly, inevitably as doom itself. Dan Darrin had not yet looked up; his nerves and his muscles were slower tuned than hers. He would not have time to look up before the bucket dropped upon his head.

Ruth, in that instant of time, saw the whole tragedy of it. The tar-pot was heavy with tar; it would strike Dan squarely; it would surely crush in his head, destroy him. And her heart went so sick within her that she could not stir. She could not breathe; she could only watch that black bucket like doom descending. Dan Darrin would be killed before her eyes; it were better that she herself should die. Why? Why? She knew the answer—and all within that space of two seconds or less. Why was she sick at heart at his peril? Because she loved him! That was why.

Then the bucket struck a line, and was deflected, and fell upon the deck six feet from Dan; and the world swam before her. She saw Dan look up to the white face of the man on the yard, and bawl: "You swipe! Come down and scrub away that mess. And sharp!" And the man came tumbling placatingly down the stays, and dropped to the deck, and Dan cuffed him to his task. By that time Ruth had her life back again; her cheeks were still white, her lips still and trembling, but—she could live, for Dan was safe.

And she loved him!

He was going right on with their talk, where he had let it fall when the man's cry came down to them.

"Yes," he said, "the sunset's all you say. Beautiful enough. But—there's no life in it, no pith. It's quiet, calm. It's sleep, or death—the death of the day. Give me the rising sun, when the world takes fire from it. It spurs you, and drives you. When the sun sets, I want to go to bed." He smiled at his own words. "When it's rising, I want to drink, or fight, or make love to a woman." And his cheeks reddened at that.

Ruth wanted to get away from him. She could not trust her tongue; it would betray her She said huskily: "Then I'm going to come up and see the sun rise in the morning. Will you let me come?"

He said: "Of course. I'll be on deck then, too."

She fled from him, so swiftly that he was concerned, and wondered if he had hurt her. But she, face down on her bunk in her cabin, was thinking: "He said it made him want to make love to a woman. And I said I'd come up and see it with him. Oh, will he think I meant he must make love to me?"

She was disturbed and unhappy over that, until she began to wonder how he knew he wanted to make love to women as the sun rose. Had he ever done it? Who was the woman? And—how dared the man have done this thing?

"I won't go on deck in the morning," she told herself.

But she did.

The sunrise was what Dan had promised her it would be. The calm had held through the night; and the sea was burnished like bronze, over its blue, when the first light stole across the water. Dan on the quarter wondered whether the girl would come. Probably not. She would sleep through it all, drowsily warm and soft. He smiled as he thought of her, sleeping.

But she was not asleep. She was awake, telling herself she would not go up to the deck, and dressing as swiftly as nimble hands could manage her garments. Before the first gray of the sky had begun to warm with rose, Dan saw her at the top of the companion, a white shadow in the white light of morning.

He called to her softly. "You did come. I thought you would sleep through."

She said: "Yes, I came."

"And in time, too! The best of it is before the sun comes clear of the sea."

She looked to the east. "How long will that be?"

"Twenty minutes—or maybe half an hour."

"Then I needn't have hurried." She was managing a steady voice. But she was so full of the thing she had discovered yesterday that she could hardly breathe. They moved together to the after rail, where they could look out between the starboard and the stern boats. She caught his eye, once, in a sidewise glance; and he was smiling. Why? She became furiously crimson. He was laughing at her; he had remembered! He thought she had come for that.

He said: "When there's one low cloud, a dark one, it's finer. To-day the line of the sea is like the line of a knife's blade."

She nodded, looking off to that blue-bronze line against the warming colors of the sky. He was watching her, not the sky. She pointed up to where a star still gleamed; and they saw its cold light wiped out by the warm brush of the coming sun. "You see," she told him, "your sunrise is death too—death of the stars, and of the night."

He shook his head. "No; the night is death, and the stars are ghosts. When the sun comes, the night wakes into life, and forgets the stars."

She said, watching him: "I never heard you talk like that. You are—quiet, when others are around."

"I told you the sunrise did things to me," he laughed. And something trembled in her. Was he beginning? Would he never begin? There was no reservation in the flooding tide of the love she had for him. Now that she knew it for what it was, she could not hold it back. And—his eyes were hers. She was in them; she could see herself in them. It was not that he did not care.

"You're cold," he said, looking at her in a way she could not understand. She shook her head.

"No, no, don't talk about me," she answered. Her guards were down with that; she felt that she had laid herself open. She had betrayed herself by that appeal. She dared not look at him.

Dan watched her; and then he said huskily: "I want to talk about you."

She could no longer think, no longer wonder, no longer fight. She could only hold her tongue, pray that he might not guess she wished him to go on. Whether he guessed or not, he did go on. "Will you let me? Don't be—angry, if I do."

She said through stiff lips: "See! There's the sun!"

He did look where she pointed, long enough to glimpse the first red rim above the distant sea. Then his eyes swept back to her. He said:

"Please!"

She was furiously impatient with him. Why was the man so slow? "Please what?" she asked.

He had one of her hands; she had not known that. He kissed it, in a hurried, fumbling, unskilled way. She said: "Oh, you said you liked to do this to women—when the sun— That's all it is."

She thought she was very cool and unmoved, and that he would be crushed. She wanted him to be crushed. But—he heard her voice trembling; and he swept an arm about her. "Ah!" he cried, laughing softly. "It was you. I— Just you!"

She pressed her hands against him, straining away from him. "Who were the women you liked to—make love to?" she demanded.

That was surrender; and he knew it, and so did she. "You! Always just you. I've known I wanted to; but there never was a woman before you."

When he had kissed her, and she had kissed him, she began to cry against the rough shirt that covered his broad chest. And her tears conquered him, so that he pleaded with her to wipe them all away. So she knew she was mistress of the situation, and she looked up at him, laughingly. She said, like a little girl reciting a lesson: "My mother told me to trust a man named Dan."

Then her arm went around his neck; and they were thus when Black Pawl stepped out on deck from the companion.

They heard him and turned; and Black Pawl stared at them with frowning brows, and asked:

"Well, Ruth, shall I thrash this one for you, too?"

She said softly: "No, Black Pawl. For—I love this one."

Black Pawl still stared, till she was a little afraid of him in spite of the boast she had made; then he wrenched his eyes away from her, and swept them around the horizon, and spoke to Darrin.

"There's wind coming, Dan," he said. "Get the stuff on her; we'll be moving on."

CHAPTER X

BLACK PAWL was right. There was wind coming, and plenty of it—too much of it. It began cheerfully enough—just a brisk breeze across a sunlit sea. But the clouds that poked up above the horizon were not cheerful; and when they obscured the sun, and the rain began to drive across the *Deborah's* decks, Black Pawl had the canvas coming in. It was time. The first squall caught them under jib and topsails; and the foretopsail went with a crack and a splinter and a whipping tear of canvas. The topmast was broken off short, and dangled and slatted back and forth; and the fore rigging, thus slacked, worked itself into a swift and dangerous confusion.

Black Pawl had been careless; and he knew it, and knew the affair was fault of his and not of the mates. He was just enough to blame himself and no one else. He went forward himself, a tower of strength, and helped clear away the tangle and cut loose the wreckage and make all secure; by that time the full strength of wind and rain was lashing them, and they hove to, to ride it out. Every hatch was closed and fast; the scuttles over the fo'c'stle and steerage and cabin companions were shut and secured, and were opened only when some one came up on deck or went below. The deck-litter was stowed; life-lines were strung fore and aft; and the boats were lashed more securely on their bearers.

A whaling vessel, and even a whaling schooner, is built not for speed but for strength. The *Deborah* was cut square across the stern; and her bows were blunt, meeting at a right angle under the bowsprit. The waves struck her with shattering, jarring blows. She was heavy with her store of oil in the casks below; and she rose sluggishly to the seas. But she was stout as she was heavy; the thundering waves could not start her timbers. Given proper handling, she would ride any sea and weather any storm.

It was nightfall before all was fast and secure. Black Pawl had held the deck all day; he held it the night through, while the pressure of the gale waxed steadily, until a man could not stand without support in the face of the wind. It was like a giant's hand that pushed against their chests; they crouched to it, clutching hand-holds, taking the lee of every shelter that offered.

Some water came over the *Deborah's* sluggish bows during the first day and night. Toward dawn a mightier wave climbed bodily inboard, over the knight's-heads. The heavy windlass and bitts, made for sternest toil, broke the first force of the wave, and saved the fo'c'stle scuttle; but the cable-boxes just aft of the foremast were ripped bodily from the deck and slung back the length of the vessel like cannon-balls in the deluge of water. There was one man on deck forward. He held to the windlass till the water had passed him by. Black Pawl and his son were on the quarter, with a third man helping them at the wheel. They were all half drowned; and the wave and the cable-boxes carried away the stern boat and the spare equipment on the skids there. In the darkness Black Pawl shouted, and his son and the seaman answered. So they stuck to their task, and in an hour the black of night faded to the lifeless gray of day; and the sheeting rain lashed and bit at them.

That day through, and hour by hour, the storm grew worse. Ruth and the missionary kept the cabin, by Black Pawl's orders. The Captain never left the deck; and Dan Darrin and the mate took turns and watches with him there. At noon of that day the galley was smashed by a wave that came over the side; and thereafter plates and knives and pans sifted overside with each fresh rush of water. Black Pawl laughed in the teeth of the storm, and howled to Dan Darrin:

"She's stripped clean as a hound, now, ready to fight."

"Aye," Dan told him. "And she's a fighter."

That second night was the worst. The tempest reached its highest pitch at dusk; but there was no slackening of its strength as the night wore through. Black Pawl could only tell his mates, from hour to hour, that it was no worse. "The break will come," he shouted into the storm; and the wind whipped his words away as though it mocked and played with him.

Black Pawl ate little while the gale endured. No man could eat, on that racking, pitching deck. He kept up his strength with whisky, raw from the bottle; and the stuff burned into his blood and warmed him and numbed him.

Dan Darrin remonstrated with him more than once. "Let that be; and put red victuals into you, sir," he urged. But Black Pawl laughed at him.

"This is my meat," he told Dan, lifting the bottle. "This is mine; you stick to yours."

Dan had never seen him so strong, so powerful and so sure. It was as though he fought the fury of wind and sea, alone, breasting the tempest for the sake of those aboard the schooner, and protecting them with his own strong body. It was like a personal triumph in battle for Black Pawl when on the third morning the wind perceptibly slackened, and the ravenous teeth of the waves became blunted and dull.

Nevertheless all that day and all that night the *Deborah* was rocked and swung and racked in the hammock of the seas; and it was not till the fourth day that they saw the sun through the graying clouds, and Black Pawl got a sight at her. On this last day, the Captain had eaten something; but he had not left the deck, and he had not slept. "There's land hereabouts," he told Dan Darrin when Dan protested. "I'll rest when I know just where we are — and not before."

They were able, by this time, to take some stock of the damage the storm had done. At first glimpse, the *Deborah* was a derelict, shattered and helpless. But that was to the casual and ignorant eye. True, the bowsprit was split, the foremast sprung, the rigging broken here and there, and hopelessly snarled forward. But the mainmast was as stoutly seated as before the tempest; and they were taking no water save the normal leakage of a healthy ship. The hull was sound.

"However," Black Pawl decided, when he knew what there was to know, "however, we're in no trim for the long way ahead. We'll make land, Dan, and put in a day or so in fetching her back to shape again. It's no great job; and it's got to be done."

Dan agreed with him. A whaler carries in herself everything she is likely to need in three or four years away from home, save only food and firewood. They could find shelter among the islands and repair the rigging and strengthen or replace the split bowsprit and the racked foremast. They would want sticks that could be counted on in the rough waters about the Horn.

When they got their sight at the sun, and Black Pawl pricked their location upon the chart, he nodded with satisfaction and clapped Dan on the back. "No more than half a day's run," he told the second mate. "There's shelter, and water, and islanders to help us if we need. Run her in, Dan—you and Red Pawl. I'm minded to sleep a bit before we're there."

They made the island at late dusk, but Red Pawl would not try the passage into the lagoon in the dark, and he stood off and on till morning. Then they worked in, and anchored a mile or more offshore. There was no town there—the place was little more than a coral atoll; but there were a few native huts. And there was the shelter they needed for their own security while they made their repairs. The mate set the work afoot as soon as the anchor was in the mud; and he and Dan Darrin drove them, while Black Pawl slept roundly in his cabin below.

The Captain slept the clock around, and woke at noon; and he woke in the after-grip of the whisky he had drunk. His body was burning and sick and sore; his eyes were hot as coals in his head; his lips were parched and swollen, and his mouth did not taste like his own mouth to him. He woke, and groaned, and rolled to the floor and dressed himself; and in a black mood he came out into the cabin and found whisky and drank again.

The reaction from his battle with the storm affected Black Pawl in two ways. His soul was sunk in a vast depression; he could see no light nor glory in the world. But his body was hot with the intoxication of victory, and a more tangible drunkenness. He was in a mood to damn the world; and when he saw Red Pawl, he hated his son; and when he saw Ruth Lytton, he cursed her in his heart. Sight of Red Pawl brought back his old misery of disappointment in this man whom he had fashioned. Sight of the girl brought back the memory of the picture she had made in Dan Darrin's arms. Why should it be Dan Darrin? Was he not a better man than Darrin? The girl was a fool. She could never be afraid of him, she had said. He told himself she might be taught that fear.

On deck, Black Pawl found fault with the fashion of one of Red Pawl's orders to the men; and Red answered him hotly. Black Pawl knocked him down with a furious blow. Red Pawl picked himself up and nursed his anger; and the Captain hated Red, and hated himself the more, and hated the world most of all. There was no laughter in him to-day; he was ghastly white, his eyes sunk in their sockets—not a man to cross with impunity.

The girl watched him commiseratingly; and once she came to him and said: "Cap'n Pawl, don't you want to go below, and sleep? You do need the rest, you know."

"I'm sick of sleeping," he told her curtly.

The missionary joined his urgency to the girl's. "You'll be ill, sir," he said. "You've won the fight; the ship's safe. Take your rest."

Black Pawl jeered at him. "Keep to your gods, Father," he said. "What do you know of the needs of men?"

"I know that men need God," said the missionary. "And—never man more than you, Black Pawl."

"Get out of my way," Black Pawl commanded. "I spurn your God!" And as the missionary moved quietly to one side, he added with a hint of the old mockery: "Now, there, Father. If there were a God, would He not strike me down for that blasphemy?"

"God strikes when He wills," said the missionary. "It is never necessary to dare Him."

Black Pawl's laughter was hollow; he cursed and swung away down the deck.

That was mid-afternoon. Till dark the men worked on the *Deborah's* repairs. That night Black Pawl kept his cabin. He was drinking steadily. He sought oblivion. But the liquor would not bite, and he cursed the feeble stuff, even as he poured it down his throat. He did not sleep. Once he got up and prowled through the cabin. On the cabin table there was a scarf, a light thing that Ruth Lytton had dropped there. Black Pawl lifted it and ran it through his hands, head bowed; and his thoughts were ugly. In the end his teeth set, and he tore the thing to bits in his hands.

In the morning Red Pawl came to him. The mate said they must go ashore and hew out timbers to make a rough splint for the bowsprit.

Black Pawl laughed in his face. "Aye, and ashore you'll teach my men to be rid of me, I doubt," he accused.

Red Pawl gave back no word, but there was a flat defiance in his eyes. The Captain waved his hand. "Go along," he said. "I'll send Darrin and his men as well."

"I'm not needing them," said Red Pawl.

"I say they go," Black Pawl roared at him; the mate turned away without further dissent.

When the Captain went on deck a little later, he found the boats in the water alongside, ready to start for the island. The missionary and the girl were there. The missionary came to Black Pawl and said:

"I want to go and see these natives, if you've no objection, sir."

"Go. Tell them about your God," Black Pawl laughed at him. They were all going, leaving him. He felt, suddenly, very lonely; and then he thought with a fierce and ugly triumph: "But she's not going—not the girl. She'll be here with me."

He saw that she was preparing to enter Dan Darrin's boat; and he went toward her and said, with something like entreaty in his voice: "Stay aboard with me, Ruth. Will you not?"

She smiled at him and said at once: "Of course, if you want me."

"I do," he told her.

The missionary hesitated, as though he were unwilling to leave them together. "Shall I stay?" he suggested.

"No; no, go — you and your God!" Black Pawl told him harshly. The missionary looked toward Ruth; she nodded, and he stepped down into the boat.

They watched the two craft pull away from the schooner's side. And Black Pawl saw that Spiess was at the after oar in Red Pawl's boat; and he saw Red lean to whisper to the man. The Captain's lips twisted with pain at the sight, as though Red had stabbed him. He knew, by now, that Red meant murder. Well, then, why did he not strike?

"Dan's boat is going faster; he's beating," said Ruth, at his side; and Black Pawl looked down at her, and his eyes were hot. He glanced along the deck. There were two men forward; the cook was working in the litter and wreckage of his galley. Save for these three, he and the girl were the only persons left upon the *Deborah*.

Sick of life, sick of decency, sick of hope and striving, he surrendered to the devils that besieged him. Damn the girl! She should learn to be afraid before he was done with her.

"Come below," he said to her. "I'm a mind to lie down."

CHAPTER XI

WHEN Black Pawl said, "Come below," his voice was harsh and sick and broken. The girl looked up at him briefly, her eyes sober and wistful; and then she smiled and asked:

"Do you mind? I'd like to wait and see which of them gets to the beach first. They're racing, you see."

Black Pawl took this delay as though it had been a respite. He was glad to wait, glad she had put him off. He tried to lie to himself in the matter, tried to hustle her impatiently to do his bidding. Nevertheless the relief in his heart would not be denied. He knew it for what it was, and he cursed himself for a weakling.

To her he only said dourly: "All right. But the mate's boat is the faster."

"I don't care," she told him challengingly. "Dan's is ahead, and staying ahead. And Dan has more of a load, too. More men with him that aren't rowing."

He grinned at her, and said jeeringly: "He's a wonderful Dan, you think."

"I do think he's wonderful," she agreed, and looked up at Black Pawl cheerfully. "I—love him."

Black Pawl's eyes darkened. Why should she love Dan? In his sober moments, the Captain knew Darrin for a brave and capable officer. Now he swore to himself that Dan was worthless and beneath respect. To the girl he said: "Fiddle! You talk of your love as the Father talks of his God."

Her eyes misted a little; and she nodded. "Yes, I do," she told him. "But—I don't believe He minds."

"Aye," said Black Pawl sardonically. "I've heard that tale."

"I never really understood how much it meant, how true it was, till—I knew Dan," she said softly.

Black Pawl banged the rail with his fist, as though he would smash the words she had spoken. He flung his hand toward the beach. "See, Red's overtaking him," he taunted.

"He is not," she protested. "He is trying; but he never will."

The Captain said: "I'll make a bet with you on that!"

"What will you bet?" she demanded.

"A kiss against a—cask of oil." He watched her covertly, and hated himself for the word he had said.

She did not answer him directly; she was looking toward the beach, and she said: "It's too late. See; Dan is there."

He saw the men leaping from the second mate's boat on the sand a mile away. "Aye," he said. "So—the cask of oil is yours. There's nothing better for the soft skin of your cheeks. Good sperm—"

"But I didn't take your wager," she reminded him gravely.

"If I'd won, I should have collected," he told her. "Take your winnings and be glad you won."

She looked at him, studied the drawn face and the sunken eyes of the man; and her heart welled suddenly with pity for him. He was sick on his feet, sick with the poison of fatigue and the poison of drink, and she touched his arm with sudden contrition. "Come," she said, "I shouldn't have kept you here on deck. You ought to be in bed. Come."

He was somehow disappointed, yet relieved. That they should go down into the cabin at his bidding was victory; that they should go at hers— It robbed him of this much of conquest. Also, she was not afraid of him. He wanted her to be afraid; he wanted to see panic fear in her eyes and to hear her cry out with fright. But— there was no fear in her—for him.

"I'm going to put you to bed," she said, "and make you comfortable, and put you to sleep. You're almost sick, Cap'n Pawl. You are sick, only you're so strong it takes a long time to beat you down."

"I'm needing no nurse," he said sullenly. The initiative was out of his hands. He was trying to recapture it, but he was strangely and utterly helpless.

"Oh, yes, you do," she said laughingly. "Men never know they're sick till they drop; they never want to give in. I know. My mother— My mother was—good in sickness. She knew how to take care of sick people. And so do I. You'll see."

The man thought, with a jarring abruptness, of another woman who had known how to tend the sick. He remembered, on that voyage she had taken with him, he had been ill—the only real sickness in his life. And she had tended him; and the memory of those attentions had been bittersweet to him through all these years. He thought of her, as he submitted unconsciously to Ruth's guidance.

She led him into his own cabin. "Lie down, on your bunk," she said. And when he hesitated, with a pretty air of command: "Do as I say, sir."

He sat on the edge of the bunk, and stretched his length upon it. Then he twisted upright, abruptly. The girl was taking off his heavy shoes. He said harshly: "Here! Don't you—"

"Sh-h-h!" she told him. "Be still."

This was not what he had planned. But he lay still. She unlaced his shoes, but she could not pull them off his feet. They were stiff and hard. She said, panting with the exertion of it: "You'll have to pull them off, I'm afraid. I can't."

How slight was her strength compared to his! He could break her between the fingers of one hand. Yet she was not afraid of him. He hated her, even while he submitted to her ministrations. Helplessness possessed him. Let her have her way; he would have his in the end.

When his boots were off, she drew blankets over him to the chin. "Now," she said, "your eyes. They're terribly tired. I'm going to bathe them."

He said: "Fiddle! Let me be."

She laughed and disappeared, and came back in an instant with a basin of water and a bit of cloth; and she made him lie still while she laved his hot eyelids with the cloth. He rebelled; but the touch of her hands on his forehead was infinitely soothing. He tried to believe these light touches of her fingers woke fires in him. Yet he wanted most of all to lie still, and rest, and sleep. . . .

Her fingers were so soothing on his forehead; presently she brought a larger cloth, wet in cold water, and laid it across his brow and his eyes. He jerked it away; but she protested softly:

"No, no, let it stay. It will make your head better, make you rest."

His wife, too, had had this foolish notion that there was virtue in a cold compress.

The girl was stroking his forehead lightly, with the tips of her fingers, and running her fingers through his hair, around and around, softly, on his temples.

"I think you'll go to sleep presently. It's what you need. You're so tired."

He tried to sit up; he protested. "Let be. I'm well enough. Let be."

She pressed him gently down again, smiling into his hot eyes. "No, no. Lie still, and fall asleep."

"I'm not sleepy," he answered harshly.

She laughed at that. "Don't tell such stories. You can hardly hold your eyes open. And—don't talk. Sleep."

Black Pawl hated himself for submitting; but he could do nothing but submit. Sleep rolled over him in waves, higher and higher. He was like a rock up which the tide was lapping. When the tide should cover him, he would sleep. . . . No chance, then. Yet he was so sleepy, so terribly sleepy.

The world was receding; it was gone. He was asleep—at peace.

The girl did not at first know when Black Pawl dropped into the deeps of slumber. He moved uneasily from side to side; and she continued stroking his forehead. But after a little, in his twistings, the compress was dislodged, and she saw his eyes were closed, and did not open as they had opened before.

She went up on deck for a space, and gazed off toward the shore. She could see the boats drawn up on the beach, but nothing of the men.

Presently she descended to her own cabin and began to brush her hair.

Black Pawl's slumber was fitful and uneasy and haunted by dreams. The man was too tired for restful sleep; his nerves had yielded to the girl's soft touch, but when she was gone, he twitched where he lay, and his arms and legs writhed and twisted. Now and again he groaned, and once he brushed at the cold compress with his hand.

Then, suddenly, he awoke. His head was splitting; his mouth was parched. He opened his eyes, sat up and looked about him — and remembered.

She was gone. So! She had tricked him to sleep and fled; thus had she sought to escape him. Perhaps she had signaled to the shore.

Then he heard her moving in her cabin, next to his. He swung his stockinged feet to the floor, and sat on the edge of his bunk, swaying uncertainly.

And he thought at the same time, though without knowing why, of his son. Red would be working with his men now; he would be bringing them back to the ship presently in a mood for anything. Black Pawl flung back his head. So be it! But—his own son!

The overwhelming misery of the man at thought of his son's treachery broke down his heart within him. He got up, moving softly on his unshod feet, and noiselessly opened his cabin door.

Her door was closed. He stood, gazing at it. Then he realized there was something in his hand; he looked down and saw the bottle.

He drained it and waited. But—it would not bite. Cursing himself for a weakling and a coward, he strode forward and struck her door with his knuckles.

She opened it quickly, and saw him, but did not fall back before his eyes.

"Oh," she said. "You were asleep."

"I'm awake," he answered harshly. "I'm coming in."

CHAPTER XII

BLACK PAWL had knocked at Ruth's door while she was preparing to put up her hair. It was about her shoulders now. He thought, abruptly, that with her hair thus, she looked very young, like a child—a child to be protected. It took the purpose out of him, to see her thus. He found himself thinking that his own daughter might have been like this, if she had lived; like this, with flowing hair, and sweetly curving lips, and the brave, calm eyes of a child.

She paid no heed to his words; she came out into the main cabin, braiding her hair and throwing it over her shoulder, out of the way. "Oh," she said, "I thought you were asleep. You must come back and go to sleep. You will be sick, truly."

"I was asleep," he replied. "I woke up. I can't sleep."

"I shouldn't have left you," she reproved herself. "But I didn't think you would wake up. Come, I'll put you to sleep again, and stay with you."

"I don't want to go to sleep."

She smiled at him. "You don't know *what* you want. You're deadly tired, and sick. Come."

Her hair was in a thick braid now, down her back. She looked more like a little child than ever; and he had a desire, almost overpowering, to yield, to go back, and sleep at her bidding. He fought it off, repeating stubbornly: "No, I don't want to sleep."

There were chairs by the cabin table, and she sat down in one of them and looked up at him and laughed. "What do you want, then? Do you know?"

He sat down, the table between them, and looked at her with his hot and aching eyes. He was dizzy and trembling with weakness. "How old are you?" he asked.

"Past twenty," she told him. His child, his daughter, would have been that age. "Why?"

"With your hair like that, you look like a little girl," he said thickly.

She nodded. "That's all I am. I don't feel

grown up, at all—except with Dan. Then I feel old enough to be his mother."

"Dan," he repeated under his breath, and she said softly:

"Yes, Dan Darrin."

His head swayed a little, back and forth, lowering at her. "Him you think you—love?"

"Him I do love."

"How do you know so surely?"

"Oh—I know."

"But if you're a child, how can you know?"

"I know," she repeated. "I—just know."

His eyes lowered to the table, and he thought, heavily. When he looked at her again, he asked: "Ever know many men?"

"Not many white men," she said, "except— the missionary."

Black Pawl laughed unpleasantly. "He's not a man; he's a woman."

"He's the finest and bravest of men."

"Oh, aye," said the Captain. "He's a man, after his kind."

"And I love him," she declared.

"Him too?" Black Pawl mocked.

There was an implication in his tone that

colored her cheeks; but she said nothing. Black Pawl leaned toward her. "Dan Darrin is all right," he said deprecatingly. "But—he's a boy. He's not a man grown, yet. You'd do best to pick a man."

"Dan's a man," she cried.

He shook his head stubbornly. "A good boy; but not a man yet. He needs ripening."

She said thoughtfully: "Don't you think it's natural for people to—like people of their own age?"

"Blind children, maybe. But not those who are wise. You're not overwise to throw yourself to Dan so swiftly."

She smiled at him gayly. "I'm not throwing myself at him," she said. "You're not—considerate, to accuse me of that."

"I said 'to' him, not 'at' him," he reminded her.

"Throwing myself away?" she laughed.

"Aye."

"I'll — risk that with Dan." She leaned toward him. "Please!" she said. "You know Dan is fine and good and strong. Don't try to make me unhappy—because you can't."

His eyes burned her; he struck his fist upon the table. "I'm as much a man as Dan."

She hesitated, watching him; and then she said, soberly: "Yes, you are."

Her eyes were troubled.

"I tell you." he exclaimed in a swift, harsh voice, "I tell you I'm as much a man as he! And I—" He was shaken by an abrupt confusion. "By the eternal, there's something in you that draws me, Ruth. There's something in you that cries out to me."

She did not speak; and he asked, in a tone that was half entreaty: "Have you not felt this at all?"

She told him frankly: "Yes; I like and admire you immensely, Cap'n Pawl."

He struck the table again. "I said it. Then why must you talk of this love that you say you have for Dan Darrin?"

"I love Dan; I but like you," she told him.

He flung up his hand. "Words, words. I tell you, there's something between us, you and me, more than liking. I'm not a man to be liked. Harsh, and cold, and rough with my men, God-denying, without scruple, called 'Black Pawl' for the sake of the deeds I have done. You'd not be 'liking' such a man. It's more than 'liking,' Ruth. I tell you, there's more."

She shook her head slowly. "You are—all that which you say," she agreed. "And yet—there's good in the heart of you. I like that good in you."

"I'm black to my soul," he boasted. She laughed softly.

"No man's that," she told him. "No man's that; and you least of all."

He sat back in his chair, hands palm down on the table before him, and stared at his bony fingers. And at last he flung up his head and leveled his eyes on her. "Have it so," he agreed. "Have it so, on your side. But on mine, this is no matter of liking. There's a deeper bond. I—" He leaned toward her, his face working. "Ruth, I don't know what it is," he cried appealingly. "But it's there; it's there. I'm drawn to you, pulled to you. It's there, I say."

She met his eyes, and answered: "I'm—drawn to you, too, Cap'n Pawl. There is—affection in me for you. I would do a great deal to help you."

"Ah, you love me," he cried, leaning toward her. But she shook her head.

"No, I love Dan Darrin—in that way. It may be that I love you in another—as a brother, or a father—"

Black Pawl laughed angrily. "You'll be a sister to me! Fiddle and all! I want no sisters. And—even though to you I may seem old enough for fathering, I'm not. I tell you I'm as much a boy as Dan Darrin, where you're concerned. Father! Brother! Fiddling talk!"

"Friends, then," she suggested straightforwardly. "We'll always be friends."

"I'm no hand for friends," said Black Pawl. "It's a milk-and-water word, where a man and a woman are in the matter."

She said, a little impatiently: "You're not very reasonable. And—you'd be the better for friends, Black Pawl."

He leaned back in his chair, and his eyes fell; he thought, abruptly, of his son; and a great hopelessness settled down upon the man. He did not know just what he had hoped for; he had not meant to speak thus to this girl. After all, what could he expect? Hers was the privilege to laugh at him. He was an old man, and he must accept youth's judgment upon him.

Through the current of his thoughts, he heard Marvin, the cook, come down into the cabin to get food from the captain's stores, below. He heard Ruth speak to the man, and heard them talk together. Ruth liked old Marvin; they were, in a fashion, cronies. She got up and stood and talked with him, while Black Pawl's sick thoughts ran on.

He forgot the other two were there, and thought of himself, and of Red Pawl. He was sick with the sickness of despair. He felt himself weak and shaken, and cursed himself for being weak. He thought that he had thrown himself at this child's feet, and she had laughed at him. Some day she would tell Dan Darrin, and they would laugh together at the weakness of Black Pawl. The thought was bitter, for strength was his pride and boast, and there was no living man who had seen that strength broken. All his life he had been known for a strong man and a ruthless one; and this frail girl had laughed at him. The tale would go abroad.

He did not care for that. Let men laugh; they would not laugh to his face. But the girl would laugh—she and Dan Darrin. And—would they not have the right to mock him? Was he not a jest and a joke upon the face of the waters? He was master of the *Deborah,* and master of all aboard her! Did she know that, this child? She must know; yet she was not afraid. Rather, she laughed.

He heard Marvin come up from the storeroom, and speak to the girl again. Here at least was fair target for his wrath. He stormed to his feet and toward the man. "On deck, you swipe!" he roared. "Get out o' my sight."

Marvin scuttled up the companion; and Black Pawl turned again to where the girl sat, and looked down at her with black and knitted brows. His hair was tumbled, his cheeks were lined, his eyes were sunken. He trembled weakly where he stood, and she was infinitely sorry for him, and stood up to face him, and said softly:

"Come, you're tired. Do let me put you to sleep."

"I tell you, I'm not minded to sleep," he answered thickly.

"No matter," she smiled. "You will be. It's what you need." She touched his arm. He flung her hand away.

"Mark this," he said. "You've not understood what I've been telling you. I say Dan Darrin's not to have you while I live. Is that clear to you?"

Faintly troubled, she said: "You're sick, and tired. You don't know what you say. Please lie down."

"I do know what I say. I do mean what I say. This is my ship, the *Deborah*. Nothing passes here save with my will. I say, this matter of Dan is to be forgotten—till I say the word."

She answered, eyes braving his: "You're a strong man, Cap'n Pawl. And—master of the ship. But there are some things beyond your command. I am one of them; my heart the other. We're Dan's."

"You're overly brave," he sneered.

"I am not afraid," she answered.

"You told me once you could never be afraid of me."

"I could never be afraid of you."

"Why not?"

"I do not know."

He lifted a hand in a tense, impatient gesture. "Listen," he commanded. "Your Dan is a mile away; he'll not be back this hour. None will come into this cabin save on my word. I tell you, I claim you from Dan Darrin, and I stick to that claim."

"I tell you," she said steadily, "that your strength and your claims are nothing to me. I'm Dan's."

His head lowered as he looked deep into her eyes for a flicker of panic. "You are not afraid, when I say this much to you?"

"No."

The strength of her, the cold courage, the steady gaze, maddened him. For a long instant their eyes met and held; then he turned away from her, walked aimlessly across the cabin, turned by the companion to look back at her. His lips moved as though there were a bitter taste in his mouth, and the girl found herself longing to run to him, to comfort him and quiet him and bid him rest. She dropped her eyes, that he might not see this tenderness in them, and turned slowly back to her cabin.

It was no more than three paces from where she stood to her cabin door. But as she reached the door, she heard him moving; and she turned in the doorway and looked at him.

He was coming toward her slowly; his eyes were bitter and angry, and he stumbled as he came.

She waited in the open door. Within arm's-length of her he stopped, swaying. He felt himself checked by a spiritual wall about her that barred him out. For a space he could not stir. He did not speak; she said no word, For seconds they stood thus, unmoving.

Then Black Pawl cursed. "Hell's fire!" he muttered, and dropping his great hands upon her shoulders, he pushed her slowly backward, into her narrow cabin. Once inside, he thrust her from him, and she caught and steadied herself against the cabin wall. He swung the door shut, then setting his shoulders against it, looked at her.

She met his eyes without flinching.

"Well, are you still so brave?" he demanded hoarsely, his lips twisting in a mocking smile.

"I am not afraid," she answered.

His brows knit. He asked dully: "What do you mean, child? How can you say that? How can you help fearing? Why are you not afraid?"

She dropped her eyes, as though she were thinking; and after a little she looked up at him again. "I'll tell you, if I can, Cap'n Pawl," she said.

"Tell on," he bade her. "Tell on. There's time."

"I don't know whether you will understand," she began, half to herself. "But—I believe in God. Just as all men do! Just as all men must, in their hearts, believe. I believe there is a God; I believe He is a very real God, caring for us. I believe He is caring for me. So I can never be afraid.

"And—there is another thing," she said. "I told you there is good in you, even though men do call you Black Pawl. I am not afraid of you, because of that good in you. I—understand you, perhaps, better than you understand yourself.

You are tired out, with your fighting the storm. You are unhappy for Red Pawl's sake. You are sick with—the liquor you have been drinking. It is almost true of you that you know not what you do.

"But you do know; and there is too much good in you to lie silent through the doing. It would never let you do that which you try to wish to do, Cap'n Pawl." She smiled suddenly, looking confidently up at him. "As a matter of fact," she said, "if you could have driven yourself on— But you can never do it, Cap'n Pawl. You could not. So, I am not afraid."

He had listened to her, frowning with the effort at thought; and when she ceased speaking, he remained silent, as though considering. His head was splitting with a throbbing ache; his eyes were coals. He could not think. Of all that she had said, he only understood that she was not afraid. It was like a challenge flung in his teeth. He said thickly:

"Not afraid? By the eternal, we'll try that!"

His right hand dropped on her shoulder, and he made to jerk her toward him, against his breast, but she came passively, unresisting. He caught her head in the crook of his arm and gazed down into her eyes. And then suddenly he felt a sickening shame as though he were beating a child. And she had not resisted! Why did she not resist, fight him, give him obstacles to overcome?

She remained passive; but it was hard for her to breathe. When her lungs were choking, she was forced to set her hands against his breast and push herself away from him.

He cried out at that. So! She was fighting at last. He let her go, for the exultant triumph of recapturing her. When she was free of him, he reached out and caught her shoulder again.

Under his harsh hand, the light fabric of her waist was torn. A wave of sickness at what he had done swept over him, and he dropped his hand.

And then he saw, hanging by a thin gold chain about her neck, a locket of gold. It was such a locket as he had given to his wife, long years ago.

CHAPTER XIII

WHEN Black Pawl saw the locket, his hands fell and hung limply at his sides. He stared at the little golden thing; and his eyes blurred, and he brushed his knuckles across them, and stared again.

Under his gaze, bent thus upon her throat, the girl crimsoned; she did not understand, but she saw that a change had come in the man. She was breathless, wondering and bewildered. She put up her hands to gather her waist together; and Black Pawl caught her wrists gently, and held them aside; and then he fumbled the locket in his thick fingers, and bent near her, so that his mop of iron-gray hair brushed her face. She looked down and saw that he was trying to open the locket with a blunted thumb-nail.

When the locket was open, he cried out, hoarsely. For it held, on the one side a daguerreotype of a little boy; and on the other, an old and faded photograph of a woman. A long time he gazed at it; then he closed it and lifting his eyes, looked into Ruth Lytton's eyes as he did so. She saw the black tragedy that was eating him, and touched his arm pityingly. "It's all right," she whispered. "It's all right, truly." She knew the man was broken with shame, even though she did not understand.

He was studying her with glazing eyes. His daughter! She was his daughter—his daughter, and mirror of his love of the years agone.

He tottered, as though under a succession of blows. He swayed where he stood; and abruptly he lifted his hands and cried out, in the agony of this new knowledge, and in a passionate abasement, to the God he had forgotten.

Silent, then, he seemed to listen for an answer. And when no answer came, the man's head drooped, and he turned stumblingly, and opened the door of Ruth's cabin, and went out. He dropped into a chair by the table in the cabin. His head fell forward on his crossed arms.

The girl was blankly bewildered by what had passed. There was no fear in Ruth Lytton; there had never been fear in her. There was infinite charity in her for Black Pawl's sins.

And—she knew the man was not himself, was half sick, was broken.

The matter of the locket meant nothing to her. She supposed that sight of it had evoked some ancient memory, but she had no guess as to what that memory might be. Standing alone in her cabin,—he had closed the door behind him,—she was trembling at the thought, not of her own peril, but of the terrible remorse and abasement in Black Pawl's cry to God. She had never seen a man thus completely broken and helpless before the Unseen; and there was a majesty about the sight that gripped her.

Nevertheless, after a moment, she felt a quite human anxiety. She had seen the full depths of Black Pawl's self-contempt; she was suddenly afraid that the man would harm himself. And when she thought of the chance of this, she forgot everything else in her haste to find him, and comfort him, and tell him all was well.

She opened the cabin door to come out; she saw Black Pawl at the table, his head dropped on his hands.

She was, at first, a little awed by this sight of a strong man crushed. Then the woman in her cried out with soft compassion; and she crossed quickly and stood beside him and touched his head.

"It's all right," she told him softly. "It's all right, Cap'n Pawl."

She could think of nothing else to say.

His shoulders shook with a convulsive tremor; and she knew that he was crying, crying like a child, with his head upon his arms. A woman's tears confuse a man; but a man's tears frighten and appal a woman. Ruth was shaken by the knowledge that Black Pawl was sobbing; she did not know what to do. She could only plead: "Please! Please don't! It's all right, truly."

With a curious abruptness he was calm. He lifted his head and looked up at her. His face was streaked with tears; and yet it was strangely serene. It was haggard, and yet it was at peace. There was none of the old mockery in his eyes, and none of the evil. It was as though his tears had washed him clean. He looked up at her; and she smiled at him, hand on his hand, and pleaded:

"Don't be unhappy!"

He was studying her countenance, line by line.

And after a moment, he said in a quiet deep voice that was unlike him:

"Will you sit down? Across the table there? I want to talk with you."

She said, "Of course," and she crossed and sat down facing him. Again, for a little, he did not speak. Then he held out his hand.

"Will you let me see your locket?" he asked.

She unclasped the chain about her throat, and passed chain and locket across to him. He held them in his hands for a moment; then he opened the locket and looked long at the two pictures inside, and there were tears in his eyes again. She asked softly:

"What do they mean to you?"

He did not answer her question; he asked one of his own. "Ruth, where did you get this locket?"

"My mother gave it to me," she said.

"Who was your mother?"

"Anna Lytton."

He touched the daguerreotype in the locket. "Who is this?"

"My brother," she told him. "He died before I was born."

"And who is—this other?" He touched the photograph of his wife.

"My mother."

He hesitated; then he asked: "Is it a—good picture of her?"

"Oh, yes. It was taken before I was born. But it was very like her."

The man wetted his lips with his tongue. "Who was your father?" he asked.

"His name was Michael Lytton."

"What was he like?"

The girl shook her head. "I never knew him."

His head bowed over the locket. When he looked up again it was to ask: "Where have you lived? What was your life? Will you tell me?"

She nodded. "We—had a strange life," she said. "Ever since I was a little girl, we have lived among the islanders. My mother was a missionary; she knew how to make sick people well, and they loved her. We stayed with them always; but she always told me that when she died, I must go home."

"Home?" he asked. "Where did she say your home was?"

"She said I was to go to people named Chase, who live in a town called Hingham, in Massachusetts."

He nodded, as though he had expected this. His wife had been Anna Chase of Hingham, in the days when he wooed her.

"Do you remember any other life but this among the islanders?" he asked.

She shook her head. "No. I know we came out on a ship, Mother and I, and landed at the islands, and stayed there. I think the captain of the ship was unkind to my mother. I think we slipped away from him. But—she never told me this. It is half memory, half guess."

"You never went home while your mother lived?"

"No."

"Did she ever tell you why?"

"She said her work was in the islands, that she could not leave them."

"Was she happy?"

The girl considered; and her eyes were dim. "Not always," she said.

The man leaned back, resting his hands against the table-rim. "You know," he said humbly, "I wish you would talk to me. Tell me about your mother."

"What do you want to know?" she asked uncertainly.

"Everything."

There was an intensity in his voice that startled her. Nevertheless she began, obediently, to tell him of her mother. And once she had begun, there was no faltering. She was so full of things to tell, and it was so pleasant to be able to speak to one who cared to listen to these things.

They were both so absorbed that they did not hear when the boats returned to the ship. The missionary, coming a little uneasily down the cabin companion, found them still sitting at the table, facing each other; and the girl was talking swiftly and eagerly to the listening man.

When Black Pawl saw the missionary, he got up from where he sat. "Ah, Father," he said softly, "I have been waiting for you."

The missionary had an eye trained to see into the souls of men. He saw that a great change had come upon Black Pawl; and he saw that the change was good. His old eyes lighted.

"I am here," he said.

Black Pawl looked toward the girl. "Ruth," he told her gently, "your Dan is back. Go bid him welcome."

The girl started toward the companion; then abruptly remembering, she turned back to her cabin—her waist was torn. She was out in a matter of minutes, in a fresh one. The missionary had asked Black Pawl: "What is it you wish of me?" But Black Pawl signed to him to wait.

When the girl came out and saw the two men, and saw their steady faces, and the somber grief in Black Pawl's eyes, she went to the Captain's side. "Cap'n Pawl," she said to him under her breath, "you must not be unhappy. Please. You are a good man. . . . Kiss me."

He bent with a swift rush of feeling and kissed her forehead; and she smiled up at him, then turned and fled to the deck where Dan waited for her.

Black Pawl faced the missionary. He turned to the table. "Father," he said, "sit down."

The missionary obeyed. He took the chair the girl had occupied. Black Pawl sat across the table; and after a minute, he began. "I've a thing to say that is hard saying," he told the old man. "But—it has got to be told. Listen, Father."

And so, straightforwardly, he told his story. He did not excuse himself; he did not palliate that which he had meant to do. He painted it in its ugliest colors, painted himself as black as the pit. He began with the moment when he and Ruth were left alone upon the schooner; he told how each step had come to pass. And he came at last to the moment when his rough hand had torn her waist, and he saw the locket at her throat. There was no heat in the man, no hysteria. He told it baldly; and at the last said:

"So I knew she was my daughter — my daughter."

He was still, with that word. He seemed to wait upon the missionary; but the old man did not speak. Black Pawl watched him; and as he watched, into the Captain's eyes stole something of that old, hard mockery of all the world. "So,

Father!" he exclaimed harshly. "Is that not the unforgivable sin?"

The missionary looked up at him in mild surprise. "It seemed to me that Ruth had forgiven you," he suggested.

Black Pawl said hoarsely: "Oh, aye! But—there's none other like her in the world."

"If she has forgiven, there is no one else to blame you," said the missionary.

"What of God?" Black Pawl asked humbly; and the missionary looked at him and smiled a wise and kindly smile.

"You do not call him 'my God,'" he suggested.

Black Pawl shook his head. "No—no. He's mine too. There's no escaping Him. But—what will He say to this matter, Father?"

The missionary rested his hands on the table, and his eyes met Black Pawl's. "It seems to me, Cap'n Pawl, that you are a new man, reborn, this hour. Is it so?"

"Aye," said Black Pawl. "It is so."

"Then—this ugly matter. Perhaps it was God's way of awakening you."

"Harsh measures, Father."

"Harsh measures were needed, my son," said the missionary gently.

Black Pawl nodded. His eyes clouded thoughtfully; he studied the other. "Father," he said at last, "you must have guessed this thing from what I told you."

"I did guess," said the other honestly.

"Why did you not tell me?"

"I was in doubt," said the missionary humbly. "I was in doubt. But—it seemed to me that matter was in His hands."

Black Pawl nodded. "Oh, aye." Then he was still again, with his thoughts. After a time, he asked like a child seeking knowledge: "Will there be punishment, Father?"

The missionary shook his head. "I do not know. Have you not suffered?"

"I would die to wipe the thing away," Black Pawl cried passionately.

"To die is not hard," said the missionary. "It is often merely release from unhappiness and pain."

"There is nothing I would not do to wipe the thing away," amended the Captain steadily. The other lifted his hand to dismiss the thought.

"Eh, Cap'n Pawl," he said quietly, "if there is to be punishment, it will come. If there is to be a cup of atonement, it will be offered to your lips."

The two men sat thoughtfully silent for a space, upon that word; and it may have been that their thoughts took the same channel, for Black Pawl was thinking of his son when the missionary asked at last: "Will you tell Red Pawl of this?"

Black Pawl hesitated. "I do not know." And he added, after a moment: "Father, I fear Red Pawl. And—I never feared him before. I am afraid for Ruth's sake. Not for my own, by the eternal!"

"Would telling him—protect her?" the missionary asked. Black Pawl laughed bitterly.

"I've taught him never a scruple in all the world," he said. "And—for what this would mean to him—God knows!"

The old man said sternly: "Red Pawl is a charge upon your soul."

"Aye," said Black Pawl. "And heavy there!"

They said no more of Red then. The missionary asked: "You told Ruth who you were?"

Black Pawl shook his head. "No, I told her nothing. What right have I to thrust such a father on the child?"

The man of the church smiled. "There's no matter of thrusting," he said. "You are her father; and—I know Ruth. She will want to know." He got up and went purposefully toward the companion. Black Pawl came swiftly to his feet.

"No, Father!"

But the missionary was calling up to the deck, "Ruth!" She answered. "Will you come below?"

She came down the companion. The missionary took her by the hand. Black Pawl stood rigid by the table. She looked from one to the other.

It was the missionary who told her — very simply, and very briefly. Not all that was to be told, not the matter of her mother's flight from this man; that was left for a quieter hour. But he told her enough so that she must see, and believe.

When he was silent, Ruth looked at her father, and she moved slowly toward him. She wanted to clasp him close; she wanted to cry; she wanted to hold the strong man's tired head against her breast. But this girl had strength, and understanding. And she saw that Black Pawl was near the breaking-point, that his jangling nerves might give way at a wrong touch. So, when she came near him, she did not cry out and throw herself into his arms as she would have liked to do. His own arms were hanging at his sides; she took hold of them at the elbow and shook him a little, back and forth; and she laughed a choking little laugh, and she said:

"I told you I wanted you to be a father to me, Black Pawl!"

His arms went around her then, gently. His head came down; his face was buried in her hair. They did not stir; they did not speak.

The old missionary smiled, and he went on deck and left them together there.

CHAPTER XIV

BLACK PAWL and his daughter were together through that afternoon, below, in the cabin; and there they cast up the old accounts of the year. And there were times when they were unhappy; but for the most part they were very happy together. There was no more rancor in Black Pawl; he loved the world, and he loved his daughter, and he loved the memories she evoked in him. Into these few hours of life Black Pawl compressed more happiness than he had seen for twenty years; he was like a boy again, gay and youthful and mirthful. Yet was there a humility about him, and a deference.

At dusk he went on deck. Red Pawl was there, superintending the work on the bowsprit. Black Pawl looked at what was being done; and he said:

"Good work, Red!"

There was in him a desire to placate his son, to win back the old comradeship, to redeem Red

Pawl from the evil that obsessed the man. But the mate looked up at his father's words and said dourly:

"I do my work. No fear!"

Black Pawl scowled, for the old, quick anger was not entirely dead in him; nevertheless he curbed himself and turned away. Red was surprised at this. It was not like the Captain. Was his father slacking, weakening, losing his grip? He smiled furtively at his own thoughts, and his heart began to pound.

After supper Black Pawl went to his cabin, alone. He wanted to sleep; he undressed and blew out the whale-oil lamp that hung near his bunk's head, and lay down.

But there was no sleep in him; he thought of Ruth, and could not sleep for happiness; he thought of his son, and could not sleep for sorrow and concern. He thought of his wife and he spoke with her in his thoughts.

There was a great peace between him and her in this communion in the night. Black Pawl was filled with peace. Even when he thought of his son, he was not disturbed; he was only sorrowful. He no longer blamed himself so bitterly on

Red's account; he felt himself in some measure absolved. It was as though he had made an atonement; it may have been that he was pre-visioning the immediate atonement he must make. He loved Red, his son; but in his heart, he condemned the man—condemned him with the stern justice which is both justice and love.

He had a great faith that Red should never harm Ruth. It was his task to guard her; and if his strength were not sufficient, strength would be given him. There was strength in her, for that matter. Thinking of this daughter of his, he was immensely proud of her. She was a woman, even as her mother had been. He thought, without disloyalty, that she was finer than her mother. And—she would never come to harm.

But—Red? What of him? Black Pawl wondered whether to tell Red that Ruth was his sister. He put the thought away. He had a feeling that this would be cowardice and shirking, that the issue was between Red and him. He was like *Frankenstein;* Red was a monster he had himself created and for which he must take responsibility. He could not beg off.

He had somewhat the attitude of the missionary. The man of the church, guessing Ruth was Black Pawl's daughter, had yet kept silent. He had said that he felt the whole matter was in God's hands. Black Pawl thought his problem was the same. He found peace in the thought. He could do his duty as he saw it—no more.

He said softly, in the darkness, to this God he had found that day: "It's in Your hands, Sir."

And he added: "But I'll do my part of what's to be done."

So passed the night.

CHAPTER XV

AT dawn Black Pawl rose and dressed himself. Though he had not slept, he was not weary. Strength had flowed into him during the night, and happiness, and peace, and a great love of life. When light began to come through the cabin ports, he felt a hunger to be on deck, with the sea wide about him, and the wind upon his cheek. He wanted to meet the new sun with something like a prayer; he felt this new day of the world was also a new day in his life.

He dressed slowly. There was a certain lassitude upon him. He was strong, but he enjoyed tasting this strength in sips. He made no quick motions. He buttoned his garments with steady, sure fingers; he took a certain joy in merely watching the perfect functioning of these fingers of his, and he thought how wonderful an instrument is the human hand.

He liked the rough feeling of his shirt about his throat. He liked the snug belt that circled his waist. There was comfort in the harsh strength of the familiar shoes he drew upon his feet. He washed himself, and he combed and brushed his hair. He was accustomed to wear his coat loose, his shirt open at the throat; but this day he buttoned the shirt and put on a tie that he had not worn for months, and he buttoned his coat about him. He laughed at himself for doing these things. "Like a bridegroom going to his wedding," he said cheerfully. "But why not, Black Pawl? Why not?"

He had marked a hole in his woolen socks when he drew them on; and he thought Ruth would mend his socks for him now. That would be a pleasant thing. All life lay pleasantly before him—marred only by Red Pawl, his son.

He would not think of Red Pawl now. That issue might be postponed; this day was for happiness. Happiness was a new thing to Black Pawl. He wished to drink deep of it.

He went out of his cabin, and paused in the doorway and looked back at the familiar belongings. This was his farewell to them; and it may have been the man felt this was true, for he looked longer than the simple fittings of the cabin seemed to warrant, and there was a wistful twist to his smile.

In the main cabin he stopped again and looked about. Ruth's door was closed. She would be still asleep. He wanted to go in and kiss her as she slept, but he would not. Dan Darrin was in his cabin also. Asleep, no doubt! And— Black Pawl smiled; he could hear the missionary snoring softly. Even the most spiritual of men may snore. Black Pawl chuckled at the thought.

There was a book on the cabin table, which Ruth had been reading the night before. Black Pawl picked it up and looked at it, and laid it down again. His eyes roved around the familiar place. He was loath to leave it. He went reluctantly to the companion at last, and climbed to the deck.

Red Pawl was there, on the break of the quarter, talking with Spiess. The sailor had a bucket on a rope; and he and two or three of the men were scrubbing down the deck from the quarter forward. When they heard Black Pawl, the two men looked toward him, and Spiess turned to his work. Red watched his father.

The sun was just breaking above the horizon.

Black Pawl glanced toward it, cast an eye about the sky. "A fair wind, Red," he said good-humoredly. "Are you thinking we'll be ready to get away this day?"

Red studied the skies, and he bit at the back of his hand. "I don't know," he said.

"You've done the work quickly," said Black Pawl. "A good job of it."

Red looked at his father and grinned, as though the older man were lying, and he knew it.

"I'm pleased with it," Black Pawl added.

Red said: "It's well you're pleased." There was a sardonic threat in his tone. But Black Pawl ignored it; he was in no mood to take swift offense at trifles. He walked to the after rail and stood there alone; presently he came back to where Red was, and said idly:

"Red, I'm thinking I'll quit the sea after this cruise."

Red Pawl said, grinning: "Aye, you're getting old."

Black Pawl shook his head good-humoredly. "No; 'tis not that, so much. But the sea irks me. I'd like to keep my feet on dry land for a spell before I die."

"You'll find few to take on land what they take at sea," said the mate.

The Captain smiled. "Aye, the sea's rough. Maybe there's no need of so much roughness on land." And he added, looking at Red: "It's like you'll have the ship when I step out, Red."

Red looked swiftly toward where Spiess was working; but Black Pawl did not mark the glance. "It's like," Red agreed curtly.

Black Pawl turned then and considered his son with thoughtful eyes; and at last he said: "Red, I've been thinking. You and I have not always jibed as father and son should jibe."

Red looked at his father silently.

"I'm sorry for that, son," said Black Pawl. "It's not a fitting thing. Like it's been mostly my fault, too. I've not been all to you that I should, not led you as wisely as I should. I'm sorry for these things, Red Pawl."

There was no softness in Red's voice when he replied. "I've no whines to make," he said. "I can hold my end—against any man."

"I'm sorry we—fought, a space ago," said Black Pawl gently.

Red's lips drew back.

"We'll not fight again," said Black Pawl, "—not my son and I. I say, Red, that for every wrong I've done you, I'm sorry this day."

If there was an appeal in his voice, Red did not respond. There was no melting in the mate's eyes. There was only black hate; and when the father saw this in the face of the son, he turned away. He was suddenly weary.

When Black Pawl turned away from Red Pawl, he stepped down from the quarter to the main-deck. He started forward toward the waist of the ship, driven by the desire to escape that which he saw in Red Pawl's eyes.

Spiess was on hands and knees on the deck, his bucket of water by his side. As Black Pawl passed him, Spiess tipped the bucket so that a sudden flood of water poured out. Intentionally or not, it wet the Captain's shoes. Automatically, as though from long habit, Black Pawl kicked out at the kneeling man and swore at him, then passed on.

As he moved on toward the waist of the ship, his back was turned to Spiess. The man got noiselessly to his feet. He lifted the heavy bucket by the rope and swung it in a whistling, circling arc.

It came down on Black Pawl's head. If it had struck squarely, it must have crushed his skull. But it struck in such fashion that his head met the side of the bucket; and the stout pail flew to pieces under the force of the blow. It did not kill Black Pawl; it but stunned him. He was not unconscious; but his senses reeled, and he fell forward on his face.

He tried, automatically, to get to hands and knees and rise and turn; but while he was on hands and knees, Spiess leaped on his back.

Then the man drove his knife to the hilt between Black Pawl's shoulders.

CHAPTER XVI

IT was as though the blade of the knife touched a spring of life within Black Pawl. He came to his feet with a swift, fierce movement that flung Spiess off his back and sent the man sprawling to one side. Then Black Pawl turned, and stared down at him, and Spiess got up, the red knife in his hand. He watched Black Pawl; and he crouched a little, his knees bent for a spring.

Black Pawl looked at Spiess, and then he looked at his son. The mate was standing on the quarter, watching as though what passed did not concern him. Black Pawl understood, then. Red had planned this, permitted it.

Black Pawl laughed at Spiess; and then he walked slowly past the man, toward the quarter-deck. He paid no more attention to Spiess; and when the man saw this, he wiped his knife on the leg of his trousers and thrust it back into its sheath. Then he looked at Red Pawl; and when the mate said nothing, did nothing, Spiess got down on his hands and knees and went back to his scrubbing.

The other seamen, who had been sharing this work with him, and who had sprung to their feet at the first hint of the tragedy, stood in a little whispering group now, watching. All had passed so quietly; there was no word spoken now. The ship was as still as death; for Death was hovering over the *Deborah's* decks in that hour.

Black Pawl walked to the quarter; and the men saw a red stain spreading through the coat upon his back. He climbed the steps to the quarter-deck; he hesitated for a little, then turned aside and sat down on the deck, his back against the rail. Then his eyes half closed, and his head lolled on one shoulder. He might have been dead even then, for all seeming.

But he was not dead. His mind had never been so clear, so acute. His body was numb; but his brain was vividly alive. He felt no pain, felt no sensation except a warm, moist stickiness that spread down his back. Also it was a little hard to breathe. There was a bubbling in his throat, and something wet upon his lips; and when he touched his lips with a weak hand, the fingers came away red.

He saw this through half-closed eyes, still sitting there, head drooping on one side.

All had passed so quietly. This was the horror of it. There had been an instant's scuffle, then nothing. The work of the schooner was going on now. Spiess was scrubbing the deck, not looking toward Black Pawl. The mate stood against the rail idly, as though nothing had happened. The little group of men by the mainmast whispered together, their faces white. They were the only jarring note in the peaceful scene.

Black Pawl was thinking. He was thinking hard and swiftly, considering what had been done, what must be done. His thoughts covered vast spaces in seconds of time. They were racing like trained runners.

He decided that he was dying. He would be dead very soon. So! Well, he was not afraid to die—not afraid to die, so he died with clean books. But—were his books clean? There was Red Pawl—his son.

Red Pawl had killed him. This was as certain

and as true as though Red's own hand had whipped that knife between his shoulder-blades. Red had encouraged Spiess; no doubt he had promised the man protection. If proof of this were needed, the proof lay in Red's attitude now. If there were any innocence in the man, he would have struck Spiess down. Or—Black Pawl knew the mate always carried a revolver—he would have shot Spiess dead within a matter of seconds after the striking of the blow.

Aye, Red Pawl had killed him—Red Pawl, his son.

The Captain felt no surge of anger at Red Pawl, with this conclusion. He was not surprised. For—Red Pawl was as he, Black Pawl, had made him. He had shown Red the ways of violence and ruthlessness. He had taught Red never a virtue of them all, save bravery, perhaps. He had taught the boy strength, and brutality, and outrage; he had taught him cruelty; he had taught him to hate the world. He had taught him to bully men and despise all women. He had made Red into the man he was. And if Red had killed him, that too was Black Pawl's teaching. He had shown Red how to kill.

Red would be master of the *Deborah* now. He would step into Black Pawl's shoes as captain. He would enter this incident in the log. No doubt he would make it most favorable to the man Spiess. And no doubt Spiess would have a chance to escape before ever they reached port. That was to be expected; that was an essential part of the whole. Red had moved Spiess to kill Black Pawl; now Red must save Spiess from the consequences. So be it! Black Pawl had no grudge against Spiess. He hated him as little as he hated the knife Spiess had thrust between his ribs. Spiess was the instrument; Red Pawl was the murderer.

Black Pawl's senses clouded for a little; his life was ebbing. Silence still held the ship. The sun climbed higher, striking into Black Pawl's face. The wind soothed him; the circling birds squawked their unmusical cries. The men whispered by the mainmast. Spiess scrubbed on. Red Pawl leaned against the rail, watching his father die.

But Black Pawl was not yet ready to die. There were still problems to be solved; there was still life to be met and conquered. He could not die. He came slowly back to consciousness again, his mind keen and lucid and unswerving.

Red Pawl would be master of the *Deborah*. He would save Spiess from punishment. What else would he do?

Black Pawl nodded his weary head. Now he was coming to it, the crux of it all. Ruth? What of her? What would her life be, with Red the master of the schooner's tiny and constricted world? What would come to her?

There was no mercy in Red Pawl. The Captain knew that. There was no scruple in him to stay his hand. And that was Black Pawl's doing. Red was dark peril personified. He was a living threat, a red danger to the girl.

The missionary? That is to say, God? Perhaps. But—men must do their share. He had promised that he would do his share. Must God do everything?

Dan Darrin, then? Could Dan guard the girl who loved him? Perhaps—perhaps not. Dan was brave enough, strong enough. But—he was straightforward, fearless, strong, and that was all. There was no craft in him. Red Pawl might easily befuddle him, blind his eyes, strike when

Dan was off guard. And—Red had killed his father; he would scarce scruple to kill Dan Darrin.

So Dan was no sure shield. Who else remained? One by one, Black Pawl considered each expedient. And there was none that satisfied him; there was no power aboard the *Deborah* to protect the girl, once he, Black Pawl, was gone.

There was no evasion in Black Pawl, no shirking his responsibility. Red was his responsibility.

The conclusion was inescapable. There was no anger in him toward his son; there was no hatred. There was only a deep love, and a deeper sorrow and grief. He stirred where he sat; and slowly, by infinite degrees, he opened his eyes.

He saw the *Deborah*, the schooner he loved, the world he had ruled. He saw the blue sky above him, and the furled canvas on the boom. He saw the group of white-faced men by the mainmast, and he saw Spiess scrubbing grimly at the deck, oblivious of all that passed. He wondered if Dan Darrin would be coming on deck soon. Dan and the missionary and the girl must still be asleep in their cabins, below. It was as well.

He swept his weary eyes about the whole spread of deck before him; and he found Red Pawl. Red had not moved. He was still leaning against the rail, watching his father die.

Black Pawl tried to speak; but there was a bubbling in his throat, and it was hard. He conquered that handicap by sheer will to conquer; and he said in a voice that was firm enough, though it was very low:

"Red, he's killed me."

Red Pawl did not answer for a moment; then he said evenly: "Aye, he's killed you."

The Captain was mustering strength. "Come here, Red," he said. "I've—things to say. And it's hard—talking."

Red hesitated; then he came slowly across and stood above his father, looking down at him.

"He's killed me," said Black Pawl again. And Red nodded.

"I don't—mind dying." Black Pawl whispered. "But Red, I—hate to be—stuck—like a pig."

Red Pawl looked at Spiess, and back at his father again. "Aye, like a pig," he said. There was no softness in his tone, nor any relenting.

Black Pawl looked toward Spiess. "Shoot him down for me to see, Red," he murmured.

Red shook his head at that. "No. There's been enough quick death. I'll see to him, in due time—no fear."

"Shoot him," Black Pawl begged.

Red shook his head. The Captain lifted a weak hand. "Then—Red—get me my gun. In my cabin. I'll shoot him. Do that much for me."

The mate considered; then he said: "No. He'd finish you while I was below."

Black Pawl's head drooped. "Aye," he agreed. "He'd finish me." He was thoughtful, silent for a little. Red saw his shoulders heaving with the hardly won breath. Then the Captain looked wearily up at him.

"Give me your gun, Red," he whispered, "—if you'll not get mine."

Red Pawl hesitated; and he thought swiftly. He was cold and without scruple. Would this profit him? Suppose Black Pawl shot at Spiess

—and missed! Then Spiess would be an enemy to be reckoned with; he would consider Red Pawl had betrayed him. But—Red was not afraid of Spiess. He could always handle the man. On the other hand, suppose Black Pawl shot straight. Then Spiess would be out of the way. There was virtue in that; it would be convenient. It would clear his own skirts; it would remove the evidence against him. Yes, he could bear to have Spiess die. And thus—there would be justice in it, and no difficulty with the log. Black Pawl would probably miss. His hand must be weak and nerveless by this; yet he was a crack shot, had always been. There was a good chance.

He looked toward Spiess, and he winked as he caught the man's eye. That was for reassurance; it would give him a talking-point to explain that he had known Black Pawl would miss—if the Captain did miss. If he shot straight, then the wink had done no harm. Spiess went stolidly on with his scrubbing.

Black Pawl had seen his son's glance at Spiess. He read it.

Red said curtly: "All right—if you like."

He took his revolver from the pocket of his coat and held it toward Black Pawl. The Captain took it in both hands carefully.

It might not be loaded. He fumbled with the mechanism, "broke" the revolver and saw the fat cartridges in their chambers. Loaded!

So, he was ready. He looked up at Red Pawl. "Kneel down," he said. "Hold me up. I am very weak, my son."

If Red Pawl had any friends among the fates, they forsook him then. He stepped toward his father, and knelt down before him, and put his arms on Black Pawl's shoulders to draw the Captain to a sitting posture.

Their faces were not six inches apart. Black Pawl said softly: "I always loved you, son."

Red Pawl grinned sneeringly at that. While the grin was still on his face, the dying man mustered the last ounce of his strength. He lifted the revolver. He jammed the muzzle against his son's breast, and shot Red Pawl through the heart.

CHAPTER XVII

RED PAWL fell forward into Black Pawl's lap. And the Captain's arms went around his son and held him close; and the revolver fell upon the deck at one side. Close against his breast Black Pawl held the body of the son he had killed.

The muffled crack of the revolver had shattered the stillness that compassed the schooner. The men on deck cried out, they began to shout hysterically. Dan Darrin was out of his bunk at the sound, and racing for the companion, half dressed. He burst up on deck to behold Black Pawl with his dead son in his arms. He was at Black Pawl's side in a single leap; and at first he did not see that the Captain was hurt. He cried:

"What is it, sir?"

Black Pawl looked up at him, and he smiled; and he said quietly:

"Dan Darrin, you're master of the *Deborah!*"

Dan Darrin turned pale; he was tugging at

Red's body. Black Pawl said: "Let him be; let me have him till the end, Dan."

"What's happened?" Dan demanded hoarsely. "What's happened, Cap'n Pawl?"

Black Pawl looked toward where the man Spiess still knelt stolidly at his task. He said with a slow effort upon every word: "Spiess knifed me, Dan. At Red's bidding, I've no doubt. But don't log that, Dan, my boy. Spiess knifed me. And—I've killed my son. I shot Red Pawl. So you'll take the ship, and take her safely home."

Dan stared; and Black Pawl added huskily: "Take—Ruth, too, Dan Darrin. She loves you; and she's worth your love. My Ruth!"

"Let me fix you up, sir," Dan Darrin begged. "You'll be all right."

Black Pawl shook his head. "I'm near gone, Dan. Let me rest till the end." And then his eyes, looking over Dan's head, lighted proudly. The missionary, roused by the shot as Dan had been, was coming now. Black Pawl smiled at him.

"Eh, Father!" he said wearily. "There was

an atonement! The bitter cup! And — I've drunk deep, Father. I've killed my son."

The old missionary had the gift of understanding; and a part of what had passed, he understood. But—he looked to Dan Darrin with a question in his eyes, and Dan said swiftly:

"Spiess knifed the Captain. And he knew it was Red Pawl's doing; so he shot the mate."

Black Pawl shook his head. "No, Father. Not because my death was his doing. Not for that I killed him. You will—understand."

"Yes, Black Pawl," said the missionary. "Yes, I understand."

"I loved him, Father."

"I know."

"I'd no anger because he killed—me. That was due me. I'd no anger for that."

"I know," said the man of the church again.

"But—he would be master of the ship, Father. Black as he was, black as I made him, he would have been master of the *Deborah*. And that could not be."

The missionary laid his hand on Black Pawl's shoulder. "Let us take him away," he said. "Let us tend you."

Black Pawl's arms tightened around his son. "No, Father. I'll keep him—till the end."

"You're not dying," Dan Darrin cried. Black Pawl smiled, and looked toward the missionary.

"Tell him," he said; and the man of the church nodded.

"Yes, he is dying, Dan," he said.

Black Pawl asked wistfully: "And what will God say to this, Father?"

"No harsh words, Black Pawl."

"You're sure? Sure?"

"Very sure."

"I killed him in love, Father."

"I know."

Black Pawl was silent, with closed eyes for a little; and then he asked gently: "Think you, I've a right to see my girl again?"

The missionary said swiftly. "Dan, bring Ruth—swiftly."

Dan, on his feet to go, echoed Black Pawl's words with an amazed question in his voice. "His girl?" he asked.

"His daughter," the man of the church told him. The missionary stayed by Black Pawl's side, and Black Pawl, eyelids drooping, held his dead son closer in his arms. He heard Ruth's step, and looked up as she bent above him.

"Eh, sweet!" he said wistfully. "Put your hand on my head. Your fingers in my hair. Your mother—used to do so."

Black Pawl looked long at her; then his eyes closed again, and through the shut lids tears seeped, and ran down his cheeks, and dropped on the head of his son, held close against his breast. Ruth spoke to him; but he seemed not to hear her. For a little time he did not stir; but when they sought to lift Red Pawl away, his arms tightened their hold.

At the last, his eyes opened once more, and looked down upon his son. And he whispered huskily, for the breath was strangling in his lungs:

"Eh, Dan—my son! I fathered you in—love; but I bred you in hate—and rancor—and cruelty. And—I've killed you—at the last. But I always —loved you—little Dan. . . . My little—boy—"

His head fell gently forward until it rested on the head of his son. He did not move again.

CHAPTER XVIII

THE third day afterward the *Deborah* sailed away from her island anchorage. Her rigging was shipshape again; her sticks were spliced and splinted and strong for any gale. The wide seas lay ahead of them, with home at the end of the blue leagues stretching from their bow. And Dan Darrin was master, on the quarter-deck, with old Flexer as his mate.

Spiess was below, ironed, oppressed by a stupor that was like death itself. Life was done, for him, as truly as for those two, Black Pawl, and Red Pawl, his son. He wasted in his irons; he had no stomach for food; and in the second month of their slow homeward way, he died.

Before they left the island, that which remained of Black Pawl and his son they had borne ashore; and they left father and son together there, within sound of the waves upon the beach. Above them whispered eternally the strong, swift winds they both had loved.

Ruth was not unhappy in that parting; for she felt in her heart that all was forever well with them, with Black Pawl, and with his son. She could not find a reason for this faith that dwelt in her; but when she spoke of it to the old missionary, he nodded; and he said:

"I feel that too, Ruth. It is as though by Black Pawl's hand they were both redeemed."

She was happy with Dan, too. Since the day when they both had been wakened by the shot, they had not spoken of that which lay between them. But—it was in their eyes for each to see. He knew, and she knew; and in their long silences together they communed.

Dan would not speak. A reticence was upon him; he was afraid of breaking in upon her thoughts of Black Pawl. He was afraid there was no room for him in her overflowing heart until the memories had somewhat passed; and he was content to wait. There was a slow strength in him; he would be ready when she turned to him.

But—Ruth did not wish to wait. And she considered the matter, with a smile twisting the corners of her mouth; she considered it for a day, and a day, and a day; and at last she laughed softly, and nodded, as if she had made up her mind.

On the evening of the seventh day, the missionary was reading at the table in the cabin. Dan sat across from him, and Ruth was at Dan's side. Dan was writing up the log; she watched him, and smiled fondly when his big hand tightened clumsily upon the pen. At last she got up and went lightly to the companion and ascended to the deck. Dan marked her going, looked after her, and bent again to his task.

After a little, old Flexer came down from the deck and stood uncertainly at the foot of the companion. Dan looked across at him and asked:

"What's up, Mr. Flexer?"

"I don't rightly know," Flexer said, and he took off his cap and scratched his head. "Miss Ruth tell't me to come down. She looked like as if there was something in her mind."

"Ruth? What for?"

"I don't rightly know," said Flexer again; and then he heard a step behind him and moved awkwardly aside as Marvin, the cook, came down with Ruth upon his heels. Ruth stopped at the foot of the companion and looked at Dan, and at the missionary. Marvin and old Flexer stood together, uncertain and uneasy.

Dan and the missionary got up. They could not take their eyes from Ruth. There was a glory in her countenance. And while they stood, she crossed to Dan's side and looked up at him.

Dan could not speak; but the old missionary asked: "What is it, Ruth? What is in your mind?"

She took Dan's hand, and with him faced the man of the church. And she said softly, her face a lovely flame:

"This, Father. This is in my mind. If Dan—"

She could not finish, but there was no need. The missionary smiled. He stepped a little forward and so presently began to speak the old enduring words. Overhead the swinging oil lamp guttered. Flexer and Marvin watched from the shadows. And once Ruth saw Flexer standing there; and for a moment thought she saw Black Pawl himself, watching with happy eyes, with someone well beloved at his side. . . .

Then the vision dimmed, and she was answering the Father, while beneath their feet the schooner swung and lifted gently with the seas. And the sea lay fair and fine before the schooner's bows—like the years that waited for their coming.

THE END